Let's Talk About Law In Elementary School

Wanda Cassidy & Ruth Yates
Editors

Detselig Enterprises Ltd.

Calgary, Alberta, Canada

Let's Talk About Law in Elementary School
© 1998 Detselig Enterprises Ltd.

Canadian Cataloguing in Publication Data

Main entry under title:
Let's talk about law in elementary school

ISBN 1-55059-156-8

1. Law—Study and teaching (Elementary) I. Cassidy, Wanda, 1950- II. Yates, Ruth, 1944-
LB1584.L47 1998   372.83   C98-910133-9

Detselig Enterprises Ltd.
210-1220 Kensington Rd. N.W.
Calgary, Alberta T2N 3P5

Detselig Enterprises Ltd. appreciates the financial support for our 1998 publishing program, provided by Canadian Heritage and the Alberta Foundation for the Arts, a beneficiary of the Lottery Fund of the Government of Alberta.

Printed in Canada

ISBN 1-55059-156-8

SAN 115-0324

Cover design by Dean Macdonald.

Table of Contents

Acknowledgements

We are grateful to the Department of Justice, Government of Canada, for providing the initial seed money for this book. Further funds for editing and publishing support were provided by Simon Fraser University.

Our thanks go to Valerie Murdoch, Program Assistant for the Centre for Education, Law and Society, and to Eileen Mallory, Word Processing Centre at Simon Fraser University, for their help with the administrative aspects of completing the book and for their word-processing skills. Thanks go to Kathy Butts for her editorial suggestions and to Shelby Sheppard, who coordinated the editorial changes.

We wish to thank each author who shared his or her expertise and classroom experience, making it possible to "talk about law in the elementary school."

About the Authors

Wanda Cassidy is a faculty member in education at Simon Fraser University specializing in curriculum development, social studies and law education. She has taught law at the high school level, directed a provincial law-related education program and was instrumental in developing the Centre for Education, Law and Society at Simon Fraser University, where she serves as Co-Director.

Margaret Ferguson has practiced law and taught high school in Alberta and is currently teaching at the elementary level in British Columbia. She is an education consultant who has developed many law-related curriculum resources and is a regular contributor to *Law Now*, a legal information magazine published by the Legal Resource Centre at the University of Alberta.

Heather Gascoigne is Principal of Lord Nelson Elementary School in Vancouver. She has authored and produced several mock trials based on fairy tales and other classics in children's literature. She was the first recipient of the Hughes Award for Access to Justice in British Columbia.

Lois Klassen is an elementary school teacher in Yarrow, British Columbia. Her foray into law-related education began when she took the law methodology course at Simon Fraser University. She currently incorporates law education into her classroom.

Michelle LeBaron has a law degree from the University of British Columbia and a Masters Degree in Education from Simon Fraser University. She is an Associate Professor in Conflict Analysis and Resolution and Women's Studies at George Mason University in Fairfax, Virginia. She has taught and practiced widely in cultural issues and conflict resolution.

Mabel C. McKinney-Browning is the Director of the American Bar Association Division for Public Education. Her career as an educator includes teaching at Chicago Public Schools and at the University of Illinois, Chicago. She is the co-author of "Stories in Time," a K-6 Social Studies series, and has written and edited numerous publications on law, civics and social studies education.

Allan McKinnon is an Associate Professor at Simon Fraser University working in the area of Science Education and Curriculum Development. He, along with colleagues, developed the highly successful program in forensics for elementary classrooms.

Victor Robinson is a Ph.D. candidate at the Institute of Conflict Analysis and is an Assistant Visiting Professor at New Century College at George Mason University in Virginia.

Shelby Sheppard is currently a Visiting Assistant Professor of Educational Foundations at Western Washington University in Bellingham, Washington. She has a Ph.D. from Simon Fraser University in Curriculum and Instruction. She has served as a classroom teacher, administrator and curriculum consultant for the British Columbia public school system and is the author of several recent articles in philosophy of education periodicals.

Peter Williams from the Toronto Board of Education developed and helped to pilot the original unit on crime detection.

Ruth Yates is a researcher and curriculum resource developer. She holds an MA in English and an MEd with a focus on law-related education. She is co-author of *Canada's Legal Environment*, editor of *A Case for Canada* and is currently editor of an internet web site called, "The Law Connection."

Filling a Gap – Let's Talk About Law

Wanda Cassidy & Ruth Yates

Background to Law-Related Education in the Schools

In the early- to mid-1970s people across Canada and the United States began to demand increasing access to information about law – a kind of practical knowledge about law that had been, up until then, the purview of the legal profession. Coupled with this was an increasing interest in what it meant to be an active citizen in a changing democracy, particularly after the social upheaval of the 1960s. In the United States, funds were obtained from government sources to renew school civics programs – to make them more relevant and issue-based. Consequently, several major programs in the United States were initiated to support the teaching of what was termed "law-related education" – or education "about" law rather than education "in" law.

In Canada, the initiative to provide law-related education to school children was intertwined with the broader "public education movement" – the movement to provide legal education and information to adults and to increase their "access to justice." Various public legal education organizations sprang up across Canada, with funding coming from government and foundation sources. By the mid-1980s all provinces had at least one major law-related organization which focused on both public legal information as well as education about law for school children. Curriculum guides for various subject areas were changed by Ministries of Education to reflect this growing interest, classroom materials on law were developed (particularly for secondary school students), legal updating services were offered to teachers, and workshops and courses were given to educators who wished to increase their understanding of law and how to effectively teach legal concepts to children.

In British Columbia, the senior law course, offered as an elective to students in grades 11 and 12, became the most popular elective of all courses offered. Across Canada, social studies courses were modified to give law topics and themes more overt status. Other courses, such as consumer education and business education courses, also incorporated greater law content. All this meant that young people in

Canada were learning more about law through their schooling than had children in past decades. This was good news, but more was needed. At a national conference on law-related education for youth, the issue of broadening and deepening the extent and influence of law education was discussed. As one of the speakers at this conference, Wanda Cassidy observed that Canadian law-related educators needed to move forward from the "adolescence phase" of unbridled energy and rapid growth to a more "mature phase" of reflection, broadening and solidification (1989, p. 27). More and different kinds of things needed to occur if significant, long-term change was to take place. Her suggestions at that time included:

- We need to work towards implementing law-related education beginning in the early grades of elementary school and towards developing a coordinated effort from kindergarten through to grade 12 and we need to begin developing programs in law that are also aimed at those children not in the mainstream – i.e., E.S.L. children, children with special needs, delinquent and "problem" children.

- We need educational organizations with existing mandates in education to assume their responsibility in law-related education. For example, university faculties of education need to be more involved, as do ministries of education, school boards and teachers' federations.

- We must share our insights, our experience and our knowledge. Law-related education in Canada suffers from a dearth of information about what people are doing and from a dearth of critical reflection. We must conduct more research. We need to assess the needs of the field carefully, develop programs based on these studies, evaluate their effectiveness and publish our findings.

This book, *Let's Talk About Law in Elementary School,* is one attempt to address a portion of each of these recommendations. Since the late 1980s there has been a growing interest from teachers at the elementary level in addressing legal topics, concepts and skills with their students. Of those teachers who enroll in our courses on law education in the Faculty of Education at Simon Fraser University, over half are elementary teachers. The public legal education organizations which still exist in Canada report a similar interest on the part of teachers of younger children. As an edited volume, this book also addresses the need for law-related educators to share information and knowledge of pedagogy. It also reflects the commitment of the Centre for Education, Law and Society at Simon Fraser University to help further law-related education in schools across Canada.

Overview of this Book

Elementary teachers who teach their students about law do so primarily through the core subjects of social studies, language arts and science, as well as through the powerful influence of the informal curriculum. Teachers, however, are generally left on their own to develop appropriate resources or to modify existing curriculum materials developed on law for more senior grades. There is still a dearth of appropriate resources and support services for elementary teachers who wish to address legal themes, concepts and processes in their classrooms. Out of this vacuum came the idea for this book.

The book is practical rather than theoretical in orientation, although theory (as it informs practice) is discussed. Each contributor to the book is active in law-related education, either at the public school level, at the program administration level or at the post-secondary level. Each author has been carefully selected to cover a range of disciplines and a variety of pedagogical approaches. All of the strategies discussed in the book have been classroom tested.

The opening chapter discusses why and how law should be taught to elementary-aged children, arguing for a conceptual, issue-based curriculum on law as critical to students' understanding of the broader picture of law's role in a democratic society. Chapter 2 traces the development of law-related education in the United States and discusses current trends, particularly in the area of law education for elementary students. As the "LRE" movement knows no national boundaries, materials, concepts and program ideas have been shared across North America since the impetus towards law education for children began in the 1970s. In Chapter 3 the authors, experienced conflict mediators, show how knowing and practising the skills and processes of law can help children avoid or resolve conflicts. Chapter 4 addresses the powerful effect of the informal curriculum and the need for educators to establish classrooms which model legal and democratic principles. The following six chapters outline different ways for incorporating law education into various subject areas: addressing legal issues through story drama; using literature to learn law-related concepts; experiencing the processes of law through games and simulations across subject areas; using law-related issues to address critical thinking in social studies; and exploring the law through forensics in science classes.

In the end it is hoped that elementary teachers will come away with a better understanding of what to stress when developing a law-related curriculum for students, as well as some practical ways that they can do this through various subject areas and in how they structure their classrooms.

Other Law-Related Resources and Support Services for Elementary Teachers

While there are still some excellent classroom resources and support services for teachers in the area of law-related education, overall the quantity of materials has diminished, as has the variety of services and organizations offering specific support.

In the last few years every public legal educational organization in Canada has suffered funding cutbacks. This has been due primarily to government dollars being allocated to debt reduction and to priorities other than education. Provincial law foundations, a major source of funding for law-related education projects, have fewer dollars to allocate as a result of declining interest rates. Consequently, the dream envisioned by many who participated in the National Conference on Legal Education for Youth in the late 1980s for increased resources and help for all levels of the school system, as well as increased funding for such areas as research, has not been realized. Instead, law-related organizations have had to concentrate on some areas and not others, eliminate certain services and charge user fees for programs previously provided for free.

Below, we outline some of the major resources teachers can still access for help in developing their law programs. These range from public legal education organizations, to government departments, to professional groups, to community agencies, to universities. In our discussion, we refer to print, audio-visual and internet resources, teacher education programs and legal updating services, field trip opportunities, resource people who may act as guest speakers in classrooms and the availability of program development assistance. In some cases, we include specific names of organizations, phone numbers and addresses. Readers, however, are encouraged to check this information as phone numbers and addresses do change. Where specific names of organizations, addresses and phone numbers are not included, readers are encouraged to contact their local public library, which has reference books outlining information on community resources, government agencies and other educational services. When seeking specific phone numbers and addresses of provincial and federal government departments, the colored pages of the telephone book provide a good source of information.

Public Legal Education Organizations

Most provinces still have at least one major public legal education organization, although many of the services once offered have been reduced. As each organization varies with the type of services offered, educators are encouraged to contact their local organization for information. For example, the Legal Services Society of B.C. no longer has a Schools Program, which for 15 years developed excellent curriculum materials for schools, held workshops for teachers and produced a bimonthly newsletter for teachers across Canada. Teachers who formerly relied on this service are now reduced to accessing Legal Services' reference library, which houses curriculum materials, legal pamphlets and news clippings, or borrowing from their collection of audio-visual materials. Similarly, the Law Courts Education Society of B.C. is no longer in a financial position to develop a wide range of new publications for schools on court and justice issues, and now must charge a fee to school classes who wish to visit the court or conduct a mock trial in a court setting.

Public Legal Education and Information Organizations

Alberta

Legal Studies Program
University of Alberta
Faculty Extension
University Extension Centre
8303 112th Street
93 University Campus N.W.
Edmonton, Alberta T6G 2T4
Tel: (403) 492-5732
Fax: (403) 492-1857

British Columbia

Law Courts Education Society
Court House
221-800 Smithe Street
Vancouver, British Columbia
V6Z 2E1
Tel: (604) 660-9870
Fax: (604) 775-3476

Legal Services Society
Suite 1500, 1140 West Pender
Street
Vancouver, British Columbia
V6E 4G1
Tel: (604) 601-6000
Fax: (604) 682-7967

The People's Law School
150-900 Howe Street
Vancouver, B.C. V6Z 2M4
Tel: (604) 688-2565
Fax: (604) 331-5401

Manitoba

Community Legal Education
Association
501-294 Portage Ave.
Winnipeg, Manitoba R3C 0B9
Tel: (204) 943-2382
Fax: (204) 943-3600

New Brunswick

Public Legal Education and
Information Service of
New Brunswick
P.O. Box 6000
Fredericton, New Brunswick
E3B 5H1
Tel: (506) 453-5369
Fax: (506) 457-7899

Newfoundland

Public Legal Information of
Newfoundland
P.O. Box 1064, Station "C"
5th Floor, Atlantic Place
215 Water Street
St. John's, Newfoundland A1C 5M5
Tel: (709) 722-2643
Fax: (709) 722-8902

Northwest Territories

Law Line
4916-47 Street
P.O. Box 1320
Yellowknife, Northwest Territories
X1A 2L9
Tel: (403) 920-2360/920-6161
Fax: (403) 873-5320

Nova Scotia

Public Legal Education Society of
Nova Scotia
911-6080 Young Street
Halifax, Nova Scotia B3K 5L2
Tel: (902) 454-2198
Info. Line and Lawyer Referral
Service (902) 455-3135 (Metro)
1-800-665-9779 (Toll free in
Nova Scotia)
Fax: (902) 455-3105

Ontario

Community Legal Education
Ontario
119 Spadina Ave, Suite 600
Toronto, Ontario M5V 2L1
Tel: (416) 408-4420
Fax: (416) 408-4424

Justice for Children and Youth
Suite 405, 720 Spadina Avenue
Toronto, Ontario M5S 2T9
Tel: (416) 920-1633
Fax: (416) 920-5855
Email: jfcy@web.net

Prince Edward Island

Community Legal Information
Association of Prince Edward Island
P.O. Box 1207
Charlottetown, PEI C1A 7M8
Tel: (902) 892-0853
Fax: (902) 368-4096
Email: cliapei@web.net

Quebec

Barreau du Québec
445 boulevard Saint Laurent, S215
Montréal, PQ H2Y 2Y7
Tel: (514) 954-3459
Fax: (514) 954-3462

Commission des Services Juridiques
2, Complexe Desjardins
Tour de l'Est, Bureau 1404
Montréal, Québec H5B 1B3
Tel: (514) 873-3562
Fax: (514) 873-8762

Gouvernement du Quebec
Ministère de la Justice
Direction des Communications
1200 route de l'Église, 9th Floor
Sainte-Foy, Québec G1V 4M1
Tel: (418) 643-5140
Fax: (418) 646-4449

Saskatchewan

Public Legal Education Association
of Saskatchewan
115-701 Cynthia Street
Saskatoon, Saskatchewan S7L 6B7
Tel: (306) 653-1868
Fax: (306) 653-1869
email: pleasask@web.net

Yukon

Yukon Public Legal Education
Association
c/o Yukon College, P.O. Box 2799
Whitehorse, Yukon Y1A 5K4
Tel: (403) 667-667-4305
Tel: 1-403-668-5297 (Toll Free –
in Yukon only)
Fax: (403) 668-5541

Trajet Jeunesse Montreal
1335 Mount Royal East
Montreal, PQ H2J 1Y6
Tel: (514) 521-2000
Fax: (514) 521-1166

University Law-Related Education Programs

Most Faculties of Education in Canada (and in the United States) do not offer specific programs for teachers in law education. Some universities offer courses for those teachers teaching business courses (with law components) at the secondary school level. Social studies methods courses also may refer to law topics, but do not focus on providing teachers with instructional strategies that are specifically law-related or designed to improve teachers' own knowledge of the law.

The exception is Simon Fraser University, the University of British Columbia and the University of Alberta. The Alberta Legal Resource Centre is housed in the Extension Division of the University of Alberta and offers programs and workshops for teachers on the law and instructional approaches. A number of years ago the Law Foundation of B.C. funded Simon Fraser University and the University of B.C. to develop a series of courses for teachers on law. The University of B.C. currently offers two credit courses through their social studies education department (on campus and through distance education) – one course on substantive law and the other on law-related methodology.

Simon Fraser University offers four law-related credit courses for teachers either on campus or through distance education. One course is on methods for teaching law to children from kindergarten to grade 12, another provides legal information to teachers, the third is on conflict resolution strategies for teachers and the fourth on school law (rights and responsibilities of teachers.)

Both Simon Fraser University and the University of Alberta also house an internet service which can be accessed by educators from across North America.

The Law Connection, from Simon Fraser:

http://www.educ.sfu.ca/cels

The Law Connection is geared specifically to the needs of teachers and can be used by any person with access to the Internet. The service provides:

- articles related to topical legal issues

- updates on relevant court decisions and legislation

- a discussion of community resources

- lesson plans which can be downloaded for classroom use

- a conferencing service where teachers can talk to each other and where students and teachers can ask legal professionals questions about law

- links to other appropriate law-related internet sites.

Law Connection is updated on a regular basis, with new themes added every two to three months. Past themes include: youth justice; equity and equality issues; hate crimes and the 50th anniversary of the Nuremberg Trials; land use law and housing issues; child protection concerns; native rights.

For information on this service contact the Centre for Education, Law and Society, Faculty of Education, Simon Fraser University, Burnaby, B.C. V5A 1S6; 604-291-4570; Valerie_Murdoch@sfu.ca.

ACJNET (Access to Justice Network)

URL: http://www.acjnet.org

ACJNET is sponsored by the Department of Justice Canada and coordinated by the Legal Resource Centre at the University of Alberta. This site contains directories and links to various legal information sites such as the Supreme Court of Canada, federal and provincial legislation, the Canadian Bar Association and certain public legal education organizations. Further information on accessing this site is available through the Legal Resource Centre in Alberta (address above.)

Youth Justice Education Program (YJEP) National Committee

Although this organization does not offer specific services to teachers (curriculum materials, educational programs or other services), its membership consists of a wide range of individuals and representatives of organizations who work in the area of youth justice education – youth court judges, child advocates, academics, school administrators, public legal educators, community developers. Participants were originally brought together by the Department of Justice, Access to Justice/Public Legal Education Division, and recently set up their own independent society with elected representatives from each province and territory in Canada. Information about this organization can be obtained from:

> Dr. David Oborne
> President
> Youth Justice Education Program
> c/o Coquitlam School Board
> 550 Poirier Street
> Coquitlam, B.C. V3J 6A7
> Fax: (604) 939-7828

Government Resources

Government departments at the federal, provincial and municipal levels are often a good source of legal information, particularly to provide background reading for teachers on current legal issues rather than to provide "user friendly" resources for students. Teachers dealing with issues ranging from immigration and multiculturalism, to fisheries and environmental protection, to animal conservation and dog licenses may contact the appropriate government department for information.

In seeking information from the federal government, the first step might be to phone the Reference Canada toll-free information number: 1-800-667-3355. Or, teachers could request a copy of Reference Canada's Annual Guide to Federal Programs and Services, which lists the toll-free telephone numbers of all federal departments and services and details the mandate and function of each service.

> Reference Canada Program
> Canada Communications Group
> Ottawa, Ontario
> K1A 0S5
> Telephone: (613) 941-3306
> Fax: (613) 941-3393

Information on current legislation can be obtained from:

> Canadian Government Publishing Centre
> Supply and Services Canada
> Ottawa, Ontario
> K1A 0S9

Like the federal government, provincial governments have toll-free information lines and Guides to Government Services publications. For example, in British Columbia the toll-free information line is 1-800-663-7867 and the address: Government Communications, 612 Government Street, Victoria, V8V 1X4. The contact numbers and addresses for provincial government information sources in other provinces can be obtained through the colored pages in the telephone book, or through the public library. Similarly, municipal government information can be obtained from these sources.

Community Organizations or Groups

There are many community organizations or groups that work in areas which are law-related. For example, environmental groups, immigrant advocacy groups, human rights organizations, civil liberties groups, organizations that work in mediation and conflict resolution, organizations that work with at-risk and high-need children (many of whom are before the courts), agencies that provide support to inmates in prisons, advocacy groups for people with disabilities, tenants rights groups, anti-poverty groups and so on.

Some of these agencies have a national or provincial presence, while others work solely at the local level and can be accessed usually through information housed in public libraries. Most community organizations have materials which may be adapted for use in an elementary law-related education program, and many would be willing to send a guest speaker to a classroom. Certainly learning about these programs would enrich teachers' knowledge of law-related issues.

Professional Associations and Organizations

The Canadian Bar Association and the local branches of the Provincial Bar are useful resources for teachers planning law curricula. The Canadian Bar Association coordinates Law Week across Canada each spring, for the purpose of better informing the public about how the legal system works. During this week students can become involved in such activities as mock trials conducted at a local courthouse, public speaking contests, poster competitions and essay-writing competitions. Special citizenship ceremonies are often conducted during this week, and several courthouses remain open on the weekend offering special programs and activities for the public. At other times of the year, teachers may wish to contact their local bar association to request a speaker for their classroom. Many lawyers are community-minded and see this involvement as a public service.

The RCMP and local police forces also are usually willing to work with teachers to develop programs related to youth justice or to provide speakers for classrooms. Often one or more members of a police force are designated to work with the schools, and sometimes police forces have prepared material that can be used with elementary children.

American Organizations

There are a number of excellent educational organizations in the United States that work primarily in the area of enhancing law-related education in the schools at the elementary and secondary levels. While materials and resources that deal specifically with U.S. laws are not suitable for the Canadian context, many of the strategies presented in these resources are transferable. As well, there are some resources that deal primarily with fundamental legal principles and concepts generic to democratic societies and which only require minor adaptations for Canadian use (for example, the Centre for Civic Education materials from California which deal with issues of authority, justice, privacy, citizens' rights and responsibilities.)

The Youth Education for Citizenship division of the American Bar Association acts as a coordinating body for the various law-related education programs in the United States. Teachers interested in finding out more about which programs are appropriate for their needs should contact:

American Bar Association
Special Committee on Youth Education for Citizenship
541 North Fairbanks Court
Chicago, IL 60611-3314
http://www.abanet.org/publiced
Telephone: (312) 988-5735
Fax: (312) 988-5032

Canadian teachers would also find the magazine *Update*, produced by the American Bar Association, a helpful resource as it is full of teaching ideas, discussions of teachers' own experiences in law-related education, a legal update section (although U.S. law) and a review of various workshops and educational programs offered to teachers.

Summary

Overall, then, there are only a few curriculum materials on law suitable for direct implementation at the elementary school level. This is the prime motivation behind this book, *Let's Talk About Law in Elementary School*, and a second book our Centre for Education, Law and Society is in the process of completing, *Storybook Mock Trials: Simulations and Role Plays for Children*.

Teachers wishing to develop law-related curricula are encouraged to use the resources and services provided by those public legal education organizations listed above and to connect with those services provided over the Internet. The services and materials provided by the other sources discussed above require greater adaptation by teachers – such as modification of reading level, change from a secondary to an elementary school focus, change from straight presentation of information to pedagogically engaging activities for children.

We encourage teachers to "take the plunge." Engaging students in law-related education is great fun and immensely important to their education.

CHAPTER 1
Why Teach Law in the Elementary Classroom?

Wanda Cassidy

In this chapter, Wanda Cassidy discusses the value of teaching law in elementary schools and explores the kinds of legal concepts which should be introduced to students. She begins by looking at the function of schools, because . . .

Public schools should reflect, as well as foster, those values, beliefs and aspirations that we as a society hold dear. In our democratic society, those values include the importance of persons, freedom of expression and movement, the right to privacy and security, tolerance and respect for the rights of others, as well as the benefits of contributing to the common good. Through our schools, we seek to give young people an understanding of the past and the present, and an awareness of community and global concerns, and to help them gain the skills which will enable them to contribute meaningfully to society and to live productive and fulfilled lives. We want each child to learn to think critically, to develop reasoning abilities and to communicate well through oral, written and creative expression. It is our hope that schools will enlarge and enrich the minds of our children as well as socialize them as they acquire the beliefs, attitudes and behaviors that lead to the creation of a better world. Much of what we envision for ourselves, individually and corporately, is reflected in the kinds of educational programs we as a society plan for our youth. Both the overt curriculum of the school, as well as the hidden or informal curriculum of school practices, play an important role in fostering these educational ideals.

The Educational Mandate and Law Education

Law is intricately woven into the very fabric of our democratic society. Therefore, in order to understand our society and be able to participate effectively as informed citizens, we must learn about what law is and how laws are made, enforced and changed. The late former Chief Justice of Canada, Bora Laskin, argued as early as the 1970s that education about law deserved greater prominence in Canadian schools. He said:

> It is very important to have a citizenry which is socially literate and social literacy to me involves some appreciation of the legal system. There isn't a single act that any government can do that does not have to find its source in the legal system (*Macleans*, 1977).

Similarly, every organization in society, whether a major corporation, a non-profit society, a small business or an informal social grouping, is regulated by law. Law, in fact, influences every aspect of our personal lives from birth to death, including relationships with family, friends, neighbors and strangers. Law affects where we live and our living accommodations. It gives structure to our working lives. Law affects: when, where and how we are schooled; what we can buy and sell; what we can and cannot do in our leisure activities; and so on. Law has been called the "cement" of society, or the "glue" that binds it together. Law has also been called the "grease" or "lubricant" of society, which enables harmonious interaction.

An interesting experiment that can be used with children to show law's overriding presence in the things they and others do is to ask them to examine a daily newspaper and circle all the items that are related to law. Although students may not identify all parts the first time around, after discussion, they may see that the entire contents of the newspaper, including how the information is presented, is regulated by or related to law – from the headlines to the classifieds, from editorials to advertisements, from the way movies are categorized to the subject matter of the comics. A similar exercise for younger children who do not read is to ask them to describe everything they did that morning from the time they woke up until they arrived at school, and then to talk with them about how each of these activities is influenced by law.

Indeed law is interconnected with everything we do in our private and public lives. It follows, then, that in order to act responsibly, we need to have at least a basic knowledge of those laws which affect us. In fact, as a society we claim that ignorance of the law is no excuse for illegal behavior. By the same token, the rights each citizen has under the law are meaningless unless they are known and can be exercised. This is true even for school-aged children. Hugh Kindred (1979), law professor at Dalhousie, put it this way:

> It is important that students know not only their civic responsibilities, but also their freedom of action within (our) system of government. The measure of good citizenship is not inculcated conformity, but a healthy respect for the rights of others as well as one's own, and an allegiance to orderly process, even in diversity. The character of law encourages such critical, yet constructive attitudes (p. 538).

Indeed a greater understanding and appreciation for the power, role and responsibility of the individual is gained through learning about law. Law in a democratic society seeks to balance the rights of the individual with government or corporate rights. Issues relating to personal freedoms and social responsibility, or minority and majority rights, are examined and debated each day in the courts across the country, in quasi-judicial settings such as administrative tribunals and alternate dispute settings, and in the law-making bodies of Parliament and provincial legislatures. All decisions are subject to the broad parameters articulated in the Canadian Constitution, which includes the Charter of Rights and Freedoms. It is this document which spells out the fundamental principles and freedoms we believe in and try to practice in our democracy. Ultimately, it is the "rule of law" which regulates our society, and to which all people, including law-makers and law-enforcers, are subject.

Developing a Law-Related Curriculum

Given the interrelationship of law with broad social issues and values, with government, with public decision-making processes and with interpersonal interactions, it is important to develop a curriculum for students which is issue-based and conceptual in orientation. This is as opposed to the "black letter law" approach to learning law – or what could be termed the memorization of the facts and details of various laws. The learning of specific statutes and regulations and the legal rules is what lawyers do, and the school's role is not to create "mini-lawyers."

Rather, it is important for students, even in the primary grades, to grapple with such issues as: why we need rules, whether rules should apply to everyone, what is fair or just in certain circumstances; what is legitimate authority and when it is appropriate to challenge that authority; and when courts should be relied on to solve our problems. These kinds of issues are not too complex for young students. At this level children already have a strong sense of justice or "what's fair." They have already learned important principles of communication and cooperation with other children. They have encountered boundaries which regulate their behavior in the home, school and playground. Many have suffered from prejudice and all have hopes of being heard, valued and respected.

An issue-focused law curriculum in school also would help develop important cognitive processes and critical thinking abilities in children – such as identifying relevant "evidence" or information, separating fact from fiction or recognizing bias, appreciating different perspectives, developing an argument, giving logical reasons to support a position, solving problems and resolving conflict, communicating effectively both orally and in writing. These abilities reflect important educational goals, and can be appropriately addressed through the kind of law-related curricula I am suggesting here.

Although most elementary schools do not have a discrete subject area called "law education," there are many opportunities to learn about law through existing subject areas – particularly social studies, language arts, science and "learning for living" programs. All of these subject areas include many law-related themes, topics and issues, and advocate the cultivation of the kinds of cognitive processes referred to above.

In summary, then, when developing a law curriculum, the following kinds of issues are important to address:

- ⊜ the relationship of law to fundamental human values, to democratic principles, to societal goals and aspirations;
- ⊜ the nature and importance of the rule of law to a democratic society;
- ⊜ the role law plays (or should play) in the family, school, community and the nation;
- ⊜ the roles, rights and responsibilities of citizens in law-making, law-enforcing, law-changing;
- ⊜ how, why and when laws change, and how to effect change;
- ⊜ the role of law and its limitations in conflict resolution and problem solving.

In the remainder of this chapter I address, in greater detail, some of these fundamental issues, under the headings of: understanding what law is; the nature of law; law as a people process; the law and legal procedure; law's limitations.

Understanding What Law Is

An understanding of what law is does not come from memorizing the dictionary definition: "a body of rules, whether formally passed as statutes, or customary law which a state or community recognizes as binding on its members, a code or system of rules." Although this is where one might start with young children, students come to understand what law is by seeing how it operates in context – by examining its function. Law is one tool used by a society to regulate the conduct of its people. In a democratic society, even the lawmakers themselves are subject to the laws that are passed.

Different people, though, in our society might have a different perspective on the role law plays. Jamie Cassels (1982), law professor at the University of Victoria, makes this point:

> For some, law is simply a statement of positive rules designed to resolve controversy. To others, it guides conduct as well as provides normative prescriptions and procedural methods for dispute resolution. A broader

view represents law as a process consisting of interdependent variables including rules, procedures, institutions and people. The law is also a socio-political statement. Rules do not exist apart from their social, economic and political basis and functions. As a reflection of political philosophy, law defines the order and nature of relationships in society, predicated upon a view of political, social and institutional priorities. Law regulates our affairs in such a way as to create a hierarchy of social and economic statutes. For example, a system which respects private property and promotes its accumulation and preservation will likely treat the uneven distribution of property as a necessary given. Contrarily, if property is seen as a public resource for equal sharing, the law will work to allocate goods accordingly. In this context law is not solely a legal concept; it is a social or political concept (p. 19).

Law can be viewed as either a vehicle for eliciting cooperation or for coercion; for communication or for control. How one defines law depends, to some extent, on one's philosophical perspective or political persuasion. The fact that there are different ways of looking at law is an important concept to convey to children, although in a manner sufficiently simple for them to understand. Hart (1961, p. 6-13) says that the best way to learn about law is to examine its relationship to three important questions:

- How does law differ from and how is it related to orders backed by threats?

- How does legal obligation differ from, and how is it related to moral obligation?

- What are rules and to what extent is law an affair of rules?

The issues Hart raises are important also for the learning that takes place through the informal curriculum of the school. Or, should all beliefs about respecting each other be written down as rules in order to be enforceable? For example, are the rules established for the classroom based on commonly-held moral principles, or do they rely on threats for enforcement?

The Nature of Law

While law may not be easily defined, the factors that influence law can be identified. Law is not a set of rules which never changes (as children may think), rather the law evolves and adapts as society's aims, goals and values change and as the people who write and interpret the law change with the times. A century ago, Oliver Wendell Holmes in *The Common Law* (1881), summed it up this way:

The life of the law has not been logic: it has been experience. The felt necessities of the time, the prevalent moral and political theories, intuitions of public policy, avowed or unconscious, even the prejudices which judges share with their fellow-men, have had a good deal more to do than the syllogism in determining the rules by which men should be governed. The law embodies the story of a nation's development through many centuries, and it cannot be dealt with as if it contained only the axioms and corollaries of a book of mathematics.

Rather than looking at law to understand law, students would benefit by first reflecting on the values, beliefs and aspirations we hold dear as a society, and then see how these are reflected in law, for law can be called the "mirror" of society (Waddams, 1987). For law to work it "cannot lag too far behind or move too far ahead of, the attitudes of society at large" (p. 16). For this reason laws are obeyed, not out of fear, nor because they may be written down, but because they reflect already determined societal values of right and wrong. For example, the societal value of "loving (caring for/respecting) your neighbor" is reflected in the legal principle of "not injuring your neighbor," as seen in the often quoted civil case of 1932, *Donoghue v. Stevenson* :

> The rule that you are to love your neighbor becomes in law, you must not injure your neighbor. You must take reasonable care to avoid acts which you can reasonably foresee would be likely to injure your neighbor. Who, then in law, is my neighbor? The answer seems to be – persons who are so closely and directly affected by my act that I ought reasonably to have them in mind as being affected when I am directing my mind to the acts which are called into question.

While quoting directly from this famous case may not be an appropriate strategy for teaching young children about law, nevertheless, children at all age levels appreciate the need to tell the truth (reflected in libel and slander laws or perjury penalties), value personal safety (reflected in assault laws or traffic regulations), want to be respected as special individuals (reflected in human rights laws or family and children legislation) and value fairness (reflected in the right to be heard by an impartial adjudicator and the right to express one's point of view). Any value that students say is important to them will be evidenced in various ways in the law. This can be a starting point for children to learn about law.

But although law and morality are interrelated, as children grow more sophisticated in understanding law, they learn that law and morality are not the same. Law, for example, can be created by fiat, or be based on the arbitrary decision by one or a few, whereas morality cannot. Morality can and does, in many ways, supersede law. Taylor (1968), in trying to tease out this relationship, writes:

> (people) sometimes, and in fact often, do feel a moral obligation to do or refrain from doing what law prescribes or forbids, but this only shows that

laws and morals at points overlap. Law in no sense depends upon morals for its existences or its validity (p. 11).

Each year the press reports on cases of conflict between someone's beliefs and the law. The blockade of logging roads is one example of environmentalists' conflict with the law based on their greater concern for the environment. Or, we see pro-life advocates willing to violate bubble zones around abortion clinics because they believe a greater evil is being committed.

Law differs from morality in another sense in that law can be used as an instrument of tyranny or to reinforce the fundamental freedoms expected of life in a democracy. The former apartheid regime in South Africa is an example of law used by a few to maintain control over the many. Hitler used law to enforce his will and contravened every basic human value in the process. Even in a democracy some would claim that law is used by established powers to maintain their power and privilege and to deny access to the powerless, the poor and the disenfranchised.

Issues of law and morality raise some interesting points of discussion with children. For example, in our society we look upon people like Ghandi, Sakharov or Wallenburg as heroes for disobeying the laws of their land and risking their lives for others. On the other hand, Canadian history books do not look favorably on the actions of Louis Riel, who disobeyed the law and was hanged as a traitor. Nor would every Canadian today support an illegal blockade of a ferry ship to protect fishing practices (U.S./Canadian "salmon war") or agree with environmentalists who spike trees to get their message across. And what about the rights of the minority when a majority decision runs contrary to a group's basic belief system, as we saw when Sikhs protested the rules requiring them to remove their turbans when visiting a Legion hall, or wear a hat as part of the uniform of a police officer. The issue often comes up with children as to whether there are certain fundamental rights which are applicable to all individuals in every society, and which should be enforced as law, such as the United Nations Charter on The Rights of Children. Even young children can and should grapple with these kinds of issues, at a level appropriate to their age.

Implicit within this discussion is the relationship of justice (a moral term) to law. We have a "justice system" which includes the people we elect to govern us, officers of the courts, the police, probation officers and so on. Many people believe that these people should administer "justice" when in fact what they do is administer the law. They are bound by the law and its regulations. If the majority of citizens find that the law is inadequate, too restrictive or unenforceable, it is the duty of the electorate to inform the politicians that the law needs to be revised. If the government is reluctant to take such action, the courts usually find a way to encourage the change either by making what appears to most as an unfair or "unjust" decision. Such a decision may create such a sense of moral outrage among the population that the government is forced to act or change the law. This occurred with the case of Irene

Murdoch, the farm wife who worked on the family farm for years, but got very little in the divorce settlement because the property wasn't in her name. The outrage over this decision created changes in family law legislation.

Law As a People Process

It is important for students to realize that law in a democratic country is formulated, implemented, administered and revised by people (both legal professionals and lay people). The late Justice Deschenes (1979) of the Quebec Superior Court, who wrote widely on human rights and justice issues, argued that since "law is made for people, and not people for law," flexibility in applying the law is crucial in order to meet society's needs. In a similar vein, a former Canadian Minister of Justice implied that both the judiciary and legislators must look beyond the law to see if social justice is being done. He says, in a speech to educators:

> Any set of laws and procedures, no matter how complete, requires continuous interpretation as it is applied in practice; and in actual practice those who interpret and apply the law have found it necessary to look beyond the written statutes to an ideal of justice which is taken to be the goal of the law (MacGuigan, 1983, p. 11).

The "average citizen" can also have a significant impact on the formulation of laws and their application in practice, either directly or indirectly. In a democracy people elect lawmakers who pass laws and formulate policy. Citizens then communicate with elected members of government on a variety of issues. Often it is the organized and vocal minority which has the greatest impact on lawmakers, with the majority of people remaining silent. If law was seen as "our law," then perhaps citizens would assume greater responsibility for it. Thomas Berger urges people to:

> be skeptical about law, and about the institutions of society. They can all be improved. . . . This is essentially a free society. We enjoy freedom of speech. We can criticize. . . . Far from weakening society, it (criticism) serves to strengthen it. In a free society, everyone must feel that his or her ideas are important, and if s/he has enough people who agree with these ideas, then these views may prevail (p. 19).

Even children can influence lawmakers and can help determine the kinds of law we have. Take, for example, the 13-year-old Ontario boy who drew world attention to the plight of children working in "sweat shops" in Asia and to the need for international involvement in changing child labor laws. Opportunities for children to bring about change are many, provided that teachers support children in their endeavors and help provide them with the skills they need to work effectively in community and school initiatives. A recent study of social studies students in British

Columbia (Bognar, Cassidy & Clarke, 1997) shows a decline over the past eight years in children's beliefs that they can positively influence the community, as well as a decline in an interest in voting. These results are worrisome and may be counteracted with a pro-active law-related education program.

The most significant way that children learn the power of participation, the importance of law-making and how to bring about change, is actually to participate in various school and community decisions and initiatives. We learn best by doing (Dewey, 1916) – by practising those skills and processes and testing out our knowledge in real life situations. Unfortunately, for various reasons, the school and the community are not well-integrated when it comes to curricula, and very little opportunity for community involvement is provided to students (Bognar, Cassidy & Clarke, 1997). The classroom and the school, though, provide an opportunity to learn about decision-making, governance and law-making primarily through the processes they are engaged with in their classroom and their school – through those "democratic" (or "undemocratic") activities their teachers and school principal permit and the degree of "power" students are given. Schools designed around practising democratic principles (or the contrary) present powerful learning opportunities for children (Zukerman, 1997; Giroux, 1988; Gutmann, 1987) – more effective than learning through textbooks about how to bring about political and legal change.

The Law and Legal Procedure

One only has to compare the laws of today with laws of yesteryear to see that laws change. For example, women in Canada were not entitled to vote until after the turn of this century. Conditions in prisons are less harsh than they once were and many laws have recently been enacted which protect the rights of individuals and minority groups. But even though we see the law "being and becoming," we need to ask such key questions as:

☞ Does the law adequately reflect our times?

☞ Should law guide or follow public opinion?

☞ Should law always reflect the wishes of the majority?

For example, polls indicate that the majority of citizens favor eliminating the laws that prohibit assisted suicides for the terminally ill. Legislators are reluctant to act on such a controversial issue and have chosen to leave the law as it is. Who is right, and how should decisions such as this one be made? Because law is so "intimately interwoven into the fabric of society . . . every bending and structuring of the latter involves a corresponding reaction in the fibers of the law" (Deschenes, 1979, p. 5). But change either by legislators or the judiciary usually does not happen rapidly in law. The legal system is essentially a conservative institution, based on years of tradition and practice, and formulated on time-tested rules. Change usually only occurs after concerted effort, and as a result of input by several parties. Lloyd (1970) says that we all need to be concerned with law's impact on human culture, to

> . . . strive continuously to refurbish (law's) image, to keep it bright, and to subject it to constant re-analysis so as to keep it in touch with the social realities of the period (p. 327).

The essentially "conservative" nature of law is most evident in its focus on proper procedure. It is this emphasis that provides the greatest stability and certainty to law, even when specific laws are changing. Despite the other influences on law such as judicial interpretation or public opinion, legal procedures generally remain consistent. Since law must be seen as more than the whim of those administering it, this focus helps ensure public confidence. In this respect everyone is supposed to be accorded the same procedures in law, such as the right to be heard before an impartial tribunal, the right to be informed of the charge against oneself, the right to counsel, the right to the benefit of doubt, the will to uncover the truth that is sworn to be upheld, the right to be considered innocent until proven guilty – procedures commonly referred to as due process. Katsch (1983) says that "this concern with method is one of the pillars upon which law is based . . . (the law) minimizes the risk of reaching the wrong result or convicting the innocent by specifying procedural steps to be followed" (p. 10).

Elementary children can learn some of the fundamental legal procedures through participation in mock trials, moot appeals and other simulated activities. By "doing law" children learn the value and importance of due process, hone various law-related skills including argumentation, listening, reasoning, oral communication – and also have fun in the process.

Law's Limitations

As a final point, it is important that children see the limitations on law's role in society. There is a tendency in our society to regard law as the "savior" of society – if only we passed more laws the world would get better! For many, the problems of violence in school, of youth crime, of intolerance towards others, of pollution, of panhandling – could all be solved by passing more laws and doling out harsher penalties. But the law must be viewed as only one of many vehicles to help solve societal problems, and often is it not the best vehicle.

There are good reasons to rely on methods other than the law or the court system to resolve conflict. For example, passing a law may detract from the need for the community to band together to address the source of a problem. Or, law enforcement officers may step in when a social service agency, a church organization or a school might be better able to meet the need. For instance, a person who lashes out at society because of poverty, illness or ignorance will not be helped by the legal system; they need care and support.

When the court is used as the mechanism to resolve a dispute, a solution might be reached but the underlying conflict may still be there. For example, the court may stipulate that a landlord cannot discriminate against a family with children who wishes to rent an apartment, but this law does not solve the housing crisis for poorer families nor does it change that landlord's attitude. Often the people who are discriminated against by others are the most vulnerable and least able to seek redress from an expensive and impersonal legal system. Likewise the courts may sentence a person to jail for robbery but fail to compensate the victim of the offence, or address the reasons why the offender chose to rob in the first place. In other instances the law may resolve immediate disputes but cannot solve underlying causes or the long-term problems or bring harmony to society.

In some instances, courts may even exacerbate a problem. Because our judicial system is based on an adversarial model, two sides of an issue are expressed, but usually only one side wins. Mediation (and other non-court processes), on the other hand, represent more humane methods of dispute resolution because the parties in conflict participate in the process that resolves their differences. Mahatma Ghandi, one of history's great peacemakers and a lawyer by profession, saw law's limitations and sought to go beyond legal solutions. After a long, but finally successful struggle to achieve an arbitration (non-court settlement) during his early years of practice, Ghandi (1948) said:

> Both [parties] were happy over the result, and both rose in the public estimation. My joy was boundless. I had learnt the true practice of law. I had learnt to find out the better side of human nature and to enter men's hearts. I realized that the true function of a lawyer was to unite parties driven asunder. The lesson was so indelibly burnt into me that a large part of my time during the twenty years of my practice as a lawyer was occupied in bringing about private compromises of hundreds of cases. I lost nothing thereby – not even money, certainly not my soul. (pp. 87,88)

Ghandi recognized law's frailty. Law's limitations must be appreciated, or it will be called upon to perform tasks for which it is ill-suited and called upon far too often.

Summary

What has been outlined here are some fundamental understandings about law that should be considered when planning law-related curricula for elementary-aged students. The complexity of the issues addressed will depend, of course, on the age of the children and the length and depth of the program. What is important for teachers to communicate to students is:

- that law is integral to the way our society works and how we live our lives;

- that law is not removed from our everyday lives – that it reflects what we believe in and those values that are important to all;

- that law is not a set of abstract rules, found in a book, and removed from the influence of people;

- that law cannot and should not be relied upon to solve all of society's ills;

- that law provides one means for solving conflict, but that other ways may be more effective and more durable;

- that all people should be treated equally before the law and have access to "justice."

References

Bognar, C. J., Cassidy, W., Clarke, P. (1997). *Social Studies in British Columbia: Results of the 1996 Provincial Learning Assessment*. Victoria: Ministry of Education, Skills and Training, Province of British Columbia.

Cassels, J. (1982). *Legal Process Casebook*. Victoria: University of Victoria, Faculty of Law.

Deschenes, C. J. (1979). *The Sword and the Scales*. Toronto: Butterworths.

Dewey, John. (1916). *Democracy and Education*. New York: The Free Press.

Ghandi, M. T. (1948). "An autobiography: The story of my experiments with truth." In J. C. Smith & D. N. Weisstub (Eds.) (1983), *The Western Idea of Law*. Toronto: Butterworths.

Giroux, Henry. (1988). *Schooling and the Struggle for Public Life: Critical Pedagogy in the Modern Age*. Minneapolis, MN: University of Minnesota Press.

Gutmann, Amy. (1987). *Democratic Education*. Princeton, NJ: Princeton University Press.

Hart, H. L. A. (1961). *The Concept of Law*. Oxford: Clarendon Press.

Katsch, M. E. (Ed.) (1983). *Taking Sides: Clashing Views on Controversial Legal Issues*. Guilford, CT: Dushkin.

Kindred, H. (1979). "The aims of legal education in high school." *Canadian Community Law Journal*, *3*, 20-25.

Laskin, The Honorable Mr. Justice B. (1977). *MacLean's*, *90*(4), 4.

MacGuigan, The Honorable M., Minister of Justice and Attorney General of Canada (1983). *Remarks to the Closing Session of the People's Law Conference*. Ottawa, May 24.

McIntyre, The Honorable Mr. Justice W. (1981). "The rule of law in public legal education." In E. Myers (Ed.), *Legal Education for Canadian Youth: Proceedings of a Conference*, May, 1980. Regina: University of Saskatchewan, College of Law. Ottawa: Canadian Law Information Council, 1-6.

Taylor, Richard. (1968). "Law and morality." *New York University Law Review*, *43*, 611.

Waddams, S. M. (1987). *Introduction to the Study of Law* (3rd Ed.) Toronto: Carswell.

Zukerman, Susan. (1997). *Democratic Student Involvement at the School Level: A Case Study of an Elementary School Student Council*. Unpublished master's thesis. Burnaby: Simon Fraser University.

CHAPTER 2
Educating for Civic Participation: Law-Related Education in the United States

Mabel C. McKinney-Browning

The American law-related education movement provided impetus and pat-terns for Canadian programs, and although the histories are somewhat different (in Canada public legal education programs were involved with school programs), law-related programs in Canada and the U.S. reflect similar goals and use similar methods to accomplish their ends.

Like many "innovative" curriculum areas, law-related education emerged from a call for change in the schools. Improving understanding of the U.S. Constitution and the Bill of Rights by improving the quality of practice was the focus of this change. The history of law-related education in the United States provides an interesting window into the process and policy that drives change in our schools.

Change in educational practice in the United States is often driven by crisis. The impetus for crisis may come from community perceptions of diminished achievement or concerns about global competitiveness. In the 1990s the call for change in education has been driven by pressure from the business community to improve the quality of the work force in the United States in order to assure continued competi-tiveness in the world economy. This call for change has also been shaped by the increase in violence in communities throughout the country and a growing awareness of changing norms for public behavior. The response to this call for improvement has been the establishment of educational standards throughout the elementary and secondary school curriculum, including civics and government.

In this chapter, we will take a look at the evolution of law-related education in the United States. The chapter will examine (1) the history of law-related education in the U.S.; (2) the goals and practice of law-related education in the elementary school curriculum; (3) the challenge of establishing an appropriate learning environment for law-related education; and (4) the future of law-related education as it struggles to meet the changing needs of the school community.

The History of Law-Related Education in the United States

Marking the beginning of law-related education is a challenge because the traditions of education in the United States are rooted in the use of schools as the means for educating citizens for participation in the nation's civic and political life. As the late president of the Carnegie Foundation, Dr. Ernest Boyer, noted:

> the establishment of a network of common schools in the 19th century was, in large measure, an attempt to strengthen democracy. The push for universal education was driven less by individual gain than by the desire to promote the social and civic advancement of the nation, based on the belief that we had, in this country, a rich heritage to be shared and a vision of participatory government to be sustained and strengthened.[1]

Educators used law as a way to improve instruction in American History and Government long before a recognizable practice evolved. For example, the "father of law-related education," Dr. Isidore Starr, reflected on his work as a high school social studies teacher and law student in the 1930s.

> What amazed me at the time was the effect of law-related discussions on the interest and quality of student thinking . . . I began to find the uses of law in social studies an important means of breaking through superficial textbook commentary to case study confrontations of value conflicts, the nature of decision making, and the quest for a hierarchy of values in our society.[2]

The establishment of law-related education as a curricular practice may be best marked by a series of events beginning in the early 1960s. In 1962, the National Council for the Social Studies was urged by its then vice-president, Dr. Isidore Starr, to join with the Civil Liberties Educational Foundation to develop a program for teaching the Bill of Rights. One result of this partnership was a teacher workshop at Williamsburg, Virginia, which developed a framework for the study of the Bill of Rights through the use of case studies. The next important event was a speech by the Associate Justice of the United States Supreme Court, William Brennan, to the 1962 convention of the National Council for the Social Studies calling on social

---

[1]Boyer, Ernest. "Civic Education for Responsible Citizens," *Educational Leadership*, November, 1990.

[2]Isidore Starr. "The Law Studies Movement: A Memoir," *Peabody Journal of Education*, October, 1977, pp. 6-11.

studies educators to teach about the Bill of Rights. Following this occasion, Justice Brennan hosted, along with Justice William O. Douglas, a meeting of influential citizens to discuss ways to bring about this change in schools. Attending the meeting were members of the legal community, the education community and leaders of national civic organizations. The meeting concluded with a commitment to make effective instruction about the Bill of Rights a national priority.

In 1963 and 1964 workshops were held throughout the country to promote the teaching of the Bill of Rights. Organizations established to spearhead this work included the Constitutional Rights Foundation and Law in a Free Society (now known as the Center for Civic Education) located in Los Angeles, California, and the Law in American Society Project located in Chicago. The work of these organizations led the way in shaping the dimensions of what we know as law-related education.

Leaders of these organizations approached the American Bar Association to lend its support to this curricular improvement effort in 1970. Although its commitment has been quite remarkable and is unprecedented, law-related education has served the interest of the American Bar Association to improve public understanding of the law and legal system in the United States. The Association's work began in 1971 when then-president of the American Bar Association, Leon Jaworski, established the Special Committee on Youth Education for Citizenship. The Special Committee was charged with fostering and improving education about the law and legal system in the nation's schools. A professional staff was hired to work with the committee in carrying out this task. Through a series of regional conferences conducted from 1973-1984, the Association brought leaders from the legal and educational communities together to discuss the importance of law-related education and to develop partnerships for establishing these programs in schools. Many of the state and local law-related programs which currently exist can trace their beginnings to these conferences. The American Bar Association continues to support the efforts of elementary and secondary teachers to implement quality programs in civic and law-related education through its Division for Public Education.

Throughout its history, law-related education has provided a substantive direction for the study of civics in schools. Law serves as the "glue" which connects the elements of civic education: politics, government, history, public policy and civic participation. The hallmarks of law-related education programs are the emphasis on real-world experiences, cooperative and participatory learning opportunities and substantive interactions with a broad range of legal and community resources. From developing and improving outreach to elementary schools, juvenile justice settings and communities of color to crafting curricula to meet the need for drug prevention and violence prevention programs in schools, law-related educators have been making exciting contributions to a quality curriculum.

The Practice of Law-Related Education in the Elementary School

Law-related education seemed to take hold in the secondary school through enrichments to the American History and American Government curriculum and through elective courses. The effort to engage the elementary school was more difficult. In 1978, the American Bar Association was awarded a grant from the National Endowment for the Humanities to develop models for teaching law and humanities in elementary schools. The program was "designed to create a variety of curricula for the schools to provide a sequence of experiences selected and organized to teach young children to live morally, creatively and effectively as persons who are becoming citizens of a democratically ordered society."

Seven sites from throughout the United States were selected to participate. Each developed a different model for the elementary school. For example, one site had students build a model city in their classroom. As they began to construct the city, students confronted the many legal issues which govern community actions and public policy. These students were challenged to maintain a fair and equitable distribution of the "city's" resources. Making decisions about how to design a space in which people can live together humanely and harmoniously was the implicit goal of the project. Another site focused on the development of student government in a K-6 elementary school. Students were divided into two governing units – K-2 and 3-6. Each classroom selected representatives to attend meetings which were held under the leadership of the school principal. Students became active contributors to decisions made for the school community. The program provided direct approaches for improving school climate and addressing the "hidden curriculum" of the school. The school truly modeled a community in which democratic values and strategies were promoted and practiced.

The most important achievement of the law and humanities project was the development of a learning continuum to guide curriculum development in the elementary grades. Dr. Charlotte Anderson, director of the project, in describing the continuum indicates that "it captures the growth in skills critical to civic participation in a diverse and pluralistic culture. The continuum is action oriented, reflecting the dynamic nature of law as both facilitative and participatory."[3]

This project, and its resulting continuum, helped to focus and highlight the range of opportunities available in law-related education for teaching elementary children the complex compendium of skills and content associated with the role of citizenship.

---

[3]Anderson, Charlotte C. "Promoting Responsible Citizenship Through Elementary Law-Related Education," *Social Education*, May, 1980, pp. 382-87.

Students moved away from:	Students moved toward:
perceiving law as restrictive, punitive, immutable and beyond the control and understanding of the people affected	perceiving law as promotive, facilitative, comprehensible and alterable
perceiving people as powerless before the law and other socio-civic institutions	perceiving people as having potential to control and contribute to the social order
perceiving issues of right and wrong as incomprehensible to ordinary people	perceiving right and wrong as issues all citizens can and should address
perceiving social issues as unproblematic	perceiving the dilemmas inherent in social issues
being impulsive decision makers and problem solvers who make unreflective commitments	being reflective decision makers and problem solvers who make grounded commitments
being inarticulate about commitments made or positions taken	being able to give reasoned explanations about commitments made and positions taken
being unable to manage conflict in other than a coercive or destructive manner	being socially-responsible conflict managers
being uncritically defiant of authority	being critically responsive to legitimate authority
being uncritically responsive to authority	being responsibly opposed to illegitimate authority
being illiterate about legal issues and the legal system	being knowledgeable about law, the legal system and related issues
being egocentric, self-centered and indifferent to others	being empathetic, socially responsible and considerate of others
being morally immature in responding to ethical problems	being able to make mature judgements in dealing with ethical and moral problems

Continuum of Law-Related Education

As the continuum shows, the elementary law-related education classroom offers students a range of opportunities to learn the complex skills associated with the role of citizen. Attention is given both to the skills to be learned and the context in which they will be applied.

Typically, elementary law-related education programs approach the curriculum in two ways. The first is the integration of the knowledge and skills associated with law-related education throughout the curriculum. For example, language arts has provided a rich source of opportunity to address law-related content. In "Reader's Theatre," students use drama to illustrate complex law-related issues like justice and authority. Children's literature has also been used as a way to help younger students expand their limited experience through story. Such stories can form the basis for "case study" in the elementary classroom. This strategy utilizes skills of analysis, synthesis and evaluation as students critically examine the story of the case in order to make decisions of right and wrong, injury and restitution.

Law-related education also offers the opportunity to put skills to work in solving problems. For example, fourth grade students at one school were finding it difficult to cross the street in front of their school. They discussed the problem at school, inviting a city official to share with them the process for getting a traffic signal placed at the intersection. They were told that they would have to show evidence of the problem being experienced at the crossing. Collecting information on the number of students crossing and the volume of vehicular traffic at critical times in the school day were required. The students met the challenge. Analyzing that data to draw conclusions supporting their arguments and reporting this to the city council completed the activity. Collecting and establishing a database for decision making brought into "real life" the value of mathematics. The power of information and process became clear to these young people as they applied their knowledge and skills to solve a problem in the community.

Secondly, the elementary school uses the community as a laboratory for bringing knowledge and skills together in meaningful learning experiences. For example, after learning about courts and trials, students may visit a courthouse to see the legal system in action and meet the people that make it work. Or they may work on a community service project that engages them in identifying a problem in the community, establishing links to others who are working on the same issue and helping to create and implement solutions. Or they may be trained by community members in how to mediate disputes in their school. Or a member of the community may be called on to bring special expertise or experience to a classroom discussion. Law-related education encourages teachers to consider how a particular community-based activity deepens learning. Understanding the role that the activity plays in the acquisition of knowledge, skills or attitudes to be fostered helps teachers to shape an experience that connects to learning.

The continuum of law-related education continues to serve as an excellent guideline for establishing benchmarks to elementary law-related education. Activities such as those noted previously provide teachers with opportunities to use law-related education as a focus for enriching and extending the ongoing curriculum. Not only do such activities energize and link the classroom experience to the community, they provide ways to encourage student ownership of learning and recognize student achievement. Students are empowered by these experiences because their ideas and opinions are valued and they are encouraged to inform their opinions with facts.

Another important tool for curriculum development in law-related education is the "Essentials of Law-Related Education." As the United States became increasingly immersed in the development of educational standards in the 1990s, law-related educators came together to examine the practice and revisit goals. The result of this activity was the "Essentials of Law-Related Education," a publication which reflects the efforts of our field to clearly articulate the curricular content and pedagogy which defines law-related education in schools. The "Essentials" looks at four aspects of law-related education practice – subject matter, instructional strategy and contexts, skills, and attitudes, beliefs and values.

Essential subject matter includes the study of concepts central to democracy. For example, students must be given opportunities to understand the nature and importance of justice, power, equality, property and liberty to the practice of democracy. In addition, study must include the relationship between the citizen and society, the role of government, and the tensions between ideal and reality in achieving the goals of democratic society. Essential skills include thinking or intellectual skills, communications skills and social participation skills. Essential instructional strategies include those which are student-focused, interactive, experiential and participatory. Essential attitudes, beliefs and values include fostering in students a commitment to constitutional democracy and the rule of law, respect for human rights and the responsibility of citizens to be informed, active participants in civic life. Although the scope of law-related education continues to be broad, the "essentials" provide a tool for assessing the quality and impact of programs and curriculum defined as law-related education.

The Importance of the Learning Environment

From its inception, law-related education has tried to balance the attention given to content with attention to the learning environment. Teachers have been challenged through this curriculum to provide opportunities in which students are actively engaged in the learning experience. To achieve the optimum environment, teachers have to be willing to view their role as facilitative. Power is shared between students and teachers as the learning process evolves. For example, classroom rules may be generated through a process that engages students in a collective, reflective analysis that encourages ownership and acceptance.

Establishing a classroom environment which mirrors and values the democratic practices taught throughout the law-related education curriculum is key. In elementary law-related education classrooms, the following elements promote such values.

(1) The opportunity for substantive and active participation by students.

(2) The presence of adult role models that reflect the behaviors that students should exemplify.

(3) Balancing the informal and formal curricula to insure that each is working toward the same learning goals.

(4) Maintaining a focus in the formal and informal curricula that builds on the social, political and cultural experiences of students in ways that are developmentally appropriate.

Hence, the elementary law-related education classroom is a place which establishes a culture of community in which democracy is valued and practiced throughout the school day. Teachers are encouraged to open their classrooms to the community in ways that provide balance, relevance and connection. Students are encouraged to take responsibility for learning, and for working cooperatively in decision making and problem solving.

The Future for Elementary Law-Related Education

The future for law-related education generally, and in the elementary school specifically, can best be seen through the changing demands on the school community. Schools in the United States are called on to help manage the culture of violence that permeates our society. They are called on to inform and deter the use of drugs, alcohol and cigarettes. They are called on to promote and facilitate changing community norms and values. The dynamic qualities of the law make it a likely and important vehicle to focus workable responses to such diverse curricular demands.

Four new program directions have emerged and taken shape over the past few years in the law-related education curriculum. First, mediation and conflict resolution have been "borrowed" from the legal community and "adopted" by schools as a vehicle for violence reduction and classroom management. Second, the renewed emphasis on cooperative (small group) learning in schools as a tool for building association and community in the classroom. Third, building on calls for volunteerism in the United States, community service activities have been developed as a bridge between students and the communities in which they live. Fourth, the growing attention to human rights both domestically and internationally serve to link the student with the basic role of citizens in democratic society – to work for the good of all.

Although conflict resolution programs were introduced in the early 1980s, they have been made a priority in schools as educators look for viable ways to improve student to student, student to teacher, and student to community behaviors and interactions. In *Everybody Wins: Mediation in Schools*, Suzanne Miller relates the following story:

> During her 6th grade year, Latonya was a frequent run away, a street fighter who once brought a butcher knife to school, for which she was suspended. She had frequently been a disputant and had gone through several mediations when she expressed the desire to become a mediator. Her reason: 'I've been in a lot of trouble myself and could help others.' Latonya was trained as a mediator in 7th grade and not only was an excellent mediator, she'd actually drag fighters off the street and into the school to be mediated.[4]

Latonya's experience illustrates several important results of the mediation experience in schools. Students gain personal power because they are exposed to a variety of tools for resolving disputes and the resolution of problems by their own actions. Students can also be shown the value of conflict in making change. Problems do not arise between people or in communities without cause. Making appropriate change is a way to manage a solution, not simply to react to a problem. Mediation programs have an important impact on the learning environment. When students are encouraged to take responsibility for their actions and interactions, working together to achieve success becomes part of the culture. Recently, a 5th grade pilot program in the Chicago Public Schools has shown that the skills learned in mediation translate to improved achievement in other curricular areas also.

Nothing is more essential to democracy and civic life than cooperation. Cooperative learning experiences offer opportunities for students to learn to respect and value the contributions of other students, to expand their knowledge and perspectives on issues and to develop skills for working effectively in groups. Law-related education strategies have been built on promoting cooperative learning as students work together to conduct mock trials, formulate policy and legislation in mock legislatures, and develop leadership skills through community action activities.[5]

Helping students to understand the required balance in civic life between the public good and individual rights is one of the greatest challenges faced by civic and law-related educators. Community service offers a promising strategy for meeting this challenge. Community service activities provide students with a vehicle for action, a context for understanding issues and problems, and an opportunity to share

---

[4]Miller, Suzanne, "Kids Learn About Justice by Mediating the Disputes of Other Kids," *Everybody Wins: Mediation in the Schools*, 1994, pp. 2-5.

[5]*Essentials of Law-Related Education: A Guide for Practitioners and Policymakers*, American Bar Association, January, 1995.

their own skills and act on their own knowledge. It also helps in moving students away from their egocentric, ethnocentric view of their community by opening up opportunities to work cross-culturally within the community.

Finally, as we approach the 50th anniversary of the United Nations Declaration for Human Rights, we have an opportunity to expand students' view of their responsibilities as citizens of the world community and the importance of the rule of law in maintaining stability globally. Ellen Moore, editor of the Children's edition of Amnesty International's Urgent Action Newsletter concludes that involvement in human rights activities "empower(s) children. They get a good feeling from doing something for someone. The notion is that, as young as they are, they can understand injustice and take action to address it. It's beyond politics. The children are indicating through their action that they care about the well-being of another person."

The past and future of law-related education are filled with hope. They represent a consistent and long-term effort to the address the nation's continuing charge for schools to build civic competence through education for productive citizenship. Our challenge is to help teachers (1) recognize the value of law-related education in meeting that expectation, and (2) to think creatively about how such programs can integrate content, skills and pedagogy to craft meaningful curricula. As Richard Morrell states, "If we are serious about education for the exercise of the responsibilities of citizenship . . . we need to approach [it] in a consistently interactive way, never losing sight of either knowledge and content on the one hand, or the dynamics of human empowerment on the other."[6]

Recommended Reading

Although it is not referenced in the chapter. I would like to include as a recommended reading the "Civics Framework for the 1998 National Assessment of Educational Progress." Produced by the National Assessment of Education Progress (NAEP) Civics Consensus Project, the framework will serve as the basis of our national test in civic education in 1998. The framework offers the reader a concise and highly assessable view of civic education in the United States.

---

[6]Morrell, Richard, "Liberal Education" winter issue, 1982.

CHAPTER 3
Resolving Conflict in the Elementary Classroom

Michelle LeBaron & Victor Robinson

Conflict resolution exercises can foster both understanding of and a pro-active attitude toward conflict situations. This chapter provides a framework for developing conflict resolution skills in classroom experiences and discusses the social benefits of using dispute resolution strategies.

Law is a formal, institutionalized method for resolving conflicts. When disputes arise in our complex society, it has become a common practice to turn to the courts for a resolution to the problem. Perhaps it has become too common a practice. Taking an issue to court is expensive, very time-consuming and not possible for everyone. It is, therefore, not always the best way to resolve conflict. It is, however, possible to apply legal understandings and adopt the skills and strategies that are used in the courtroom to try to resolve disputes and avoid the necessity of turning them over to the legal process. As the use of alternative dispute resolution methods grows in our society, it becomes just as important to educate our children in the use of these alternative forums as it is to educate them in the use of existing legal forums.

Mediation and other extra-legal methods of conflict resolution are increasingly being used in many settings – in divorce cases, labor disputes, public policy issues, environmental disputes and community conflicts. Accompanying the growth of these alternative methods, known collectively as ADR (alternative dispute resolution), has come an increased interest in understanding and improving the informal methods which we use to settle conflicts in our own lives every day.

In the school, alternate dispute resolution strategies are ideal for addressing the conflicts that arise among children each day. For example, children can learn to resolve their own conflicts without having to rely on an authoritative decision by an adult. Conflict resolution teaches invaluable life skills with applications and consequences far beyond day-to-day childhood conflicts, and can be also be an effective learning strategy because of its emphasis on interpersonal communication, cooperation, problem solving and self-reliance.

The most direct application of ADR in the schools takes the form of peer mediation. In peer mediation programs, students are trained to mediate disputes among other students, helping the students to communicate clearly with one another and jointly develop a solution to the conflict between them. While adults may think this is a daunting task for young children, some studies find peer mediation programs most successful at the elementary school level (e.g., Pilati, 1993). Children understand children's problems and can generate realistic solutions to them, sometimes more realistic than those imposed by adults.

Research on the effects of peer mediation programs is in its infancy, but preliminary results and anecdotal evidence suggest positive effects on school climate, reduced burden on administrative disciplinary procedures and positive impacts on students trained as peer mediators (see Lam, 1989, and Cheatham, 1988). Among the shortcomings of these programs, however, are the facts that only a limited number of students (those selected as peer mediators) receive direct skills training, and students are being exposed to only one approach to conflict resolution (mediation). Also, a growing tendency to rely on peer mediation as a disciplinary, rather than educational, tool threatens to undermine the non-coercive, collaborative values which make mediation such an empowering and effective *alternative* to authoritarian disciplinary methods.

In the following pages we will focus on the application of conflict resolution in the classroom. Conflict resolution topics can be taught in the classroom as separate lessons or infused in existing curricula; for instance, as a part of a social studies lesson, as a focus for examining themes in literature or in examples used in mathematics lessons. However, the most powerful applications come from teaching conflict resolution skills as basic life skills and applying those skills in day-to-day classroom interactions and pedagogy.

Conflict Resolution Skills

Conflict resolution involves both cognitive understandings about conflict and conflict resolution strategies and integration of basic relationship skills into students' repertoire of behaviors. Key relationship skills include communication skills, collaborative problem-solving skills and the ability to cooperate. Kreidler (1984) suggests that the following cognitive skills are also basic to conflict resolution:

1. analysis – defining the conflict
2. ideation – developing alternative solutions
3. strategy – gaining a working knowledge of conflict resolution techniques (p. 52).

These cognitive skills could be taught using more traditional pedagogical techniques, with students sitting at their desks working in isolation. Their application of these skills to real life situations, however, requires that they be integrated into the students' interactions with one another, in the context of relationships. Relationship skills are the foundation for constructive conflict resolution behavior. Teaching children how to communicate clearly and effectively and how to work together collaboratively are essential life skills and, without them, conflict resolution becomes another academic subject which will have little impact on the children's interactions with one another.

One of the most easily overlooked components of conflict resolution education is attitude change. Children often receive implicit messages that conflict is bad, that conflict is something to be avoided or suppressed, that being involved in a conflict is misbehavior. One of the essential lessons of conflict resolution is that both students and the adults who work with them must recognize that conflict is a normal inevitable part of each child's (and each adult's) life and that conflict, handled constructively, represents an opportunity for growth and positive change.

Each of these components of conflict resolution education – cognitive skills, relationship skills and attitude change – supports and reinforces the other. Without relationship skills, cognitive knowledge exists in a vacuum. Without cognitive knowledge, children (and adults) will not know how to apply relationship skills to resolving specific conflicts. Unless children are exposed to an environment in which they are supported in openly acknowledging their conflicts, they will not have the courage to apply these skills. And, to close the circle, until they have developed conflict resolution skills and cognitive understandings, it will be difficult to understand how conflict can be a positive experience in their lives.

Over and over again we see children (and adults) reacting to conflict rather than dealing with it pro-actively. Reactive behavior tends towards either pole of capitulation or aggressive confrontation. There is nothing more satisfying in conflict resolution work with children than seeing the moment when they realize that conflict is not something that just happens to them but something over which they have some control, something which they have the knowledge to think about and the skills to act upon.

Conflict Resolution Skills and Experiential Learning

Conflict resolution skills may be taught in a variety of ways, depending upon the objectives of the teacher and the needs of the students. It is important at the outset to acknowledge that the multicultural make-up of many schools means that there is no one cookie cutter approach that will work for everyone. Educators using conflict resolution exercises are well advised to adapt the materials to the specific needs of their classroom and to be prepared to listen to student feedback about the fit of the skills for them.

Conflict resolution is not a structured step-by-step process which can be taught like the mechanics of mathematical calculation. Rather, it is a way of interacting which depends on a base of interpersonal cooperation, communication and collaborative problem-solving skills. These skills, in general, are acquired through experience and developed in practice. These skills in particular can *only* be practiced in the context of relationships. An experiential approach is necessary in order for students to integrate these responses in their repertoire of social skills.

There are a number of excellent resources which provide experiential exercises to enhance conflict resolution skills in children. William Kreidler's book *Creative Conflict Resolution* is addressed specifically to elementary education. It provides exercises for teaching communication skills, anger management, cooperation and tolerance as well as cognitive understandings of conflict. *The Friendly Classroom for a Small Planet* (Prutzman, et al., 1988) describes the Children's Creative Response to Conflict Program, an experiential conflict resolution program with exercises designed around four themes of cooperation, communication, affirmation and problem solving, with an emphasis on community building in the classroom. A number of other excellent conflict resolution resources and resources addressing specific relevant skills are listed at the end of this chapter.

Practicing relationship skills should not be confined to a small period of time dedicated to conflict resolution. Social skills are best taught in natural applied settings. Teachers can encourage their positive development throughout the school day by modelling active listening, cooperation and collaborative problem-solving in their interactions with students and by allowing students ample opportunities to engage in cooperative play and learning; in other words, by creating an environment in which positive, collaborative social interactions are the norm.

With a foundation of basic relationship skills, students may begin integrating cognitive understandings of conflict and conflict resolution into their interactions. Experiential exercises can turn cognitive understanding into attitude change. Conflict curricula often start with a simple exercise, such as having students build a conflict "web," an exercise designed to surface students' own understandings of conflict. The attitude change invited in this sort of exercise involves students recognizing conflict as a category for cognitive understanding, as something which can be thought about rather than simply as a force of nature to be endured.

From there, students can be encouraged to deeper thinking about the causes of conflicts and the ways in which they react to conflict, drawing on their own experiences whenever possible. It is especially useful for teachers to keep an eye out for "teachable moments," conflicts which arise in the classroom which provide opportunities to apply students' cognitive understandings in real life situations and for teachers to model constructive conflict behavior.

Role Play and Simulations

Specific exercises can be used to develop specific cognitive and relationship skills with an ultimate goal of integrating these skills into daily classroom interactions. An invaluable pedagogical tool for integrating these skills and understandings is role play. Role plays involve simulation to provide a safe environment in which children can experiment with and reality-test conflict resolution strategies. Research suggests a number of other benefits of role plays and simulations which make them particularly appropriate in conflict resolution education.

Kissner and Beamish (1987) state that research shows that ". . . simulations do motivate and stimulate enthusiasm as well as increasing learning in the affective/attitudinal domain" (p. 3). As noted before, attitude change is an essential component of conflict resolution education. Among the educational benefits of simulation, Kissner and Beamish report that they:

- provide students with the opportunity to solve problems first-hand;

- help integrate subject matter into an experience most closely approaching real life;

- give students an opportunity to try out modes of action and interaction before having to face real life situations;

- convey a feeling for the complexity of the decision-making process and for the multiple variables required in making decisions; and

- stress the process or skill development part of learning as well as content. (p. 4)

Collaborative problem-solving and decision-making skills are required for students to set up and enact a role play. In addition to the content of the role play, the exercise itself engages the very skills we are trying to instill.

Role plays can be used to apply and reinforce cognitive concepts through experience. For instance, one of our favorite exercises in Children's Creative Response to Conflict workshops is called Big Red. It begins with a telling of the Little Red Riding Hood story in which Little Red Riding Hood, at her mother's behest, sets off through the woods to deliver dinner to her ailing grandmother. At her grandmother's house she encounters the Big Bad Wolf, who has taken the guise of Little Red's grandmother. Little Red slowly comes to realize that it is indeed the Big Bad Wolf, whom her mother had warned her about, lying in her grandmother's bed. She and her grandmother are, in the end, rescued by a passing hunter. (Participants in teacher workshops have recognized traditional gender roles in this fairy tale, and have suggested variations such as having Little Red or the grandmother take the role of rescuer.)

Following the telling of the story, the workshop leader or teacher lists each of the characters on the board and asks the class to name what each character needs. For example, Little Red needs to visit her grandmother, the grandmother needs her dinner, and the mother needs to know that her daughter is safe. With older students the list of needs becomes more cognitively complex. Little Red needs an experience of independence, the grandmother needs the company of her granddaughter, etc. Especially important is the examination of the Wolf's needs, for a central lesson of this exercise is to understand the different perspectives of participants in a conflict. The wolf may need, for instance, a good meal or a sense of power.

Once a list of needs is established, students are asked to develop, in small groups, an alternative story line in which each of the characters' needs are met without violence. The students are then asked to role play the new story line. (With younger students, the alternative story line may be developed by the whole group with the teacher's assistance.)

This exercise addresses cognitive skills – analysis and ideation (in Kreidler's vocabulary). It requires that students recognize that there are different points of view in a conflict and helps them develop empathy with all the different points of view. It stimulates them to generate creative new solutions and introduces the idea of trying to meet the needs of everyone involved in a conflict. The role play element reinforces all of the cooperative decision-making and collaborative problem-solving skills mentioned above and has the students bring together cognitive and relationship skills.

Development and Experiential Learning

Since we are discussing the use of role plays with young children, a note about developmental appropriateness is in order. Selman (1976) presents a developmental model particularly relevant to the understandings of multiple perspectives essential to conflict resolution. He identifies Stage One (ages 6-8) as social-information role taking. This stage, he states, is typified by the child who can see herself and the others as actors with potentially different interpretations of the same social situation, largely determined by the data each has at hand. The child realizes that people think differently because they may be in different situations or have different information.

Children at this stage, Selman states, are unable to maintain their own perspective and simultaneously put themselves into the place of others by attempting to judge their actions. Nor can they judge their own actions from others' viewpoints. Thus, even though children at Stage One recognize the existence of different points of view, they maintain the idea that only one is "right."

Children at Stage Two (ages 8-10) are able to understand that people think differently because each person has his or her own uniquely ordered set of priorities and values. This leads to the moral development of understanding that no person's belief is absolutely right or valid. A major development at this point is the ability to reflect on the self's behavior and motivation from the perspective of another. These reflections do not occur simultaneously, but sequentially.

Based on Selman's model, role playing would be most effective for 8- to 10-year-olds who were involved in a critical period of debriefing to facilitate mutuality of understanding between the children's points of view and the points of view of the characters who have been role played. The child at Stage Two is also able to see that others and self are multi-motivated and that therefore altruistic and self-interested motives may intersect. At this point, the question of values, of laws regulating behaviors and of the consequences of actions can be explored profitably through role playing.

Bringing the Skills Together in the Classroom

It is not enough to identify skills and plan lectures around them. If conflict resolution teaching is to be truly successful, it needs to occur in an environment where these skills are encouraged and modelled; where there is congruence between the philosophy of conflict resolution and the classroom setting, including classroom structure and rules, teacher behavior and classroom organization.

For example, if conflict resolution skills are taught in a classroom where the teacher has frequently told students, "If you cannot say something nice, do not say anything at all," then students may not feel free to use their skills of assertion and collaborative problem-solving. If conflict resolution skills are presented in an environment where there is a very hierarchical, authoritarian approach to discipline, the rules may limit the opportunities students have to use their skills and, worse, may even prevent the students from using these skills because surfacing conflict is strongly discouraged by the structure of the school.

Conflict resolution is, by design, a non-authoritarian process. It is about empowering students by providing them with skills and opportunities to confront and successfully negotiate conflicts on their own. Teachers are sometimes uncomfortable giving up the familiar sense of control provided by hard-and-fast rules and top-down discipline. If control is the major classroom objective, then the conflict resolution approach may not be appropriate. Conflict resolution approaches do not neatly coexist with authoritarian approaches to discipline.

That is not to say that a classroom organized around conflict resolution principles is "out of control." Rather, some of the responsibility for maintaining a comfortable learning environment is shifted to the students themselves. Teaching conflict resolution skills reduces the need for teacher intervention by creating a cooperative classroom environment. This reduces the level of conflict in the classroom and encourages students to address conflicts among themselves before they become disruptive.

We sometimes hear adults yearning for a small town environment where people don't need to lock their doors, where everybody knows one another and helps out in times of need. Admittedly, this picture is sometimes idealized, but within it is the kernel of the conflict resolution approach to classroom education. We are seeking to create a sense of community inside the classroom, a community where students know and trust one another, where they have skills that allow them to cooperate effectively and where they have had positive experiences of collaborative activities.

In our idealized small town, the authority figure, the local sheriff, often plays the role of problem-solver rather than enforcer. Similarly, the teacher, in a conflict resolution approach, addresses classroom conflicts by guiding students through a problem-solving process rather than by imposing a solution from above. When conflicts are constantly "resolved" by punishment or imposition of the teacher's will, students will come to rely on authority figures to resolve their conflicts and their own efforts at developing personal conflict resolution skills and strategies will be discouraged. When students understand that they have the power and opportunity to develop realistic solutions to conflicts collaboratively, reliance on teacher intervention decreases. Hopefully, as they grow older, they will be able to apply these skills as adults to adult conflicts without resorting to violence or relying on an impersonal and overworked legal system.

Application in the Classroom

Now it's time for some reality-testing. What teacher has the time to stop the class and problem-solve every time Lisa pulls on Lucretia's ponytail? And what do we do when the students are rambunctious, the teacher next door is complaining about the noise and the principal is "concerned" about our approach to discipline?

The first question is related to a larger question in the conflict resolution field. Collaborative processes, that is, conflict resolution processes which involve the efforts of all the people involved in working out a mutually satisfying solution, generally take longer than authoritative processes in which one person makes a unilateral decision for the group. The theoretical argument, difficult to prove conclusively although supported by some research, is that a collaborative decision requires more time up front but is more efficient in the long run. A collaborative process elicits the wisdom of the entire group in anticipating obstacles prior to implementation of a decision. Also, through collaborative processes, it is more likely that the people affected by a decision understand the rationale for that decision and have "bought into" it, that is, have a greater commitment to seeing it work because they have participated in constructing it. Therefore, the argument goes, collaborative solutions are more efficiently implemented and more likely to stick.

In the classroom this means that if Lisa and Lucretia take the time to work out a solution to the hair pulling (with the teacher guiding the process, if necessary), it is likely to save time in the long run by preventing further disruption of the class. In the classroom setting, there is an even stronger argument for taking the time to work through collaborative processes. The classroom is a community of individuals with daily on-going interactions. Working through a collaborative process is not just about developing a solution to the problem at hand. It is a teaching and learning process with the potential to have a long-term impact on classroom relationships. Lisa and Lucretia are not just learning how to prevent hair pulling. They are learning empathy for one another's perspectives; they are learning a process, a way of interacting, which addresses problems collaboratively; and they are developing a different kind of relationship, one which forestalls unnecessary conflict and forms a basis on which to constructively address the conflicts which do arise.

A common approach, once students become accustomed to conflict resolution techniques, is to establish a table or corner of the classroom as a conflict corner. When a student conflict becomes disruptive, the teacher can ask those students to take their disagreement to the conflict corner and work out an agreement. William Kreidler (1984) suggests that students be given three minutes to try to resolve their conflict and then to report their agreement to the teacher or, if they were not able to resolve their conflict, request that the teacher help out. Anecdotal reports from teachers and some research suggests that time spent teaching children problem-solving methods and establishing a problem-solving culture in the classroom pays off in the long run. As students become more confident in their abilities, teachers spend less time dealing with disciplinary problems.

The second question mentioned above has to do with perceptions of control in the classroom. As we pointed out earlier, a classroom organized around conflict resolution principles is not out of control although it may sometimes look that way to outsiders. The "democratic rabble" in the 18th century must have seemed out of control to the French and English monarchs as well. So what do you do with your democratic rabble when your colleagues are more comfortable with monarchy? Sorry to disappoint you, but we're going to put this question aside for now and address it after first fortifying ourselves by looking at some further benefits of conflict resolution education.

Benefits of Conflict Resolution as Education

Among the goals of conflict resolution education directly relevant to conflict behavior and understanding are to enable students to:

- understand that conflict is not necessarily something to be avoided
- learn more about conflict and conflict dynamics

- understand more about their personal responses to conflict and the effects their personal responses have on others
- identify and construct common ground when there is a conflict
- learn a simple process for approaching conflict that can work when they are in conflict with a peer or an educator
- create and assess the most viable means for resolving a conflict
- learn ways to accept responsibility for their conflict-related behavior and of encouraging peers to do the same
- form alliances with others who acquire conflict resolution skills to work towards improving the climate of the school.

Among the benefits of conflict resolution education which have wider applications in students' lives and learning are enabling students to:

- learn ways to manage their anger and other strong emotions
- analyze problems before responding out of anger or frustration
- develop negotiating skills
- identify multiple options to solve problems
- learn skills in critical and strategic thinking, questioning, active listening, assertiveness and organization.

Conflict resolution can contribute to more general educational objectives as well. Current thinking about child development and learning emphasizes the social basis of learning, that learning occurs through social interaction (e.g., see Garton, 1992, and Winegar, 1989). Celia Brownell (1989), referring to the work of Brown and Palincsar, summarizes this direction of thinking:

> These researchers typically contrast the traditional view of the child as a self-directed learner with a perspective that emphasizes the social origins of cognitive change. They posit social processes such as internalization as the mechanism of change. This work has begun to make some real progress in identifying the range of processes that mediate the effectiveness of group learning over solitary learning. Among peers these include the sharing of expertise, externalization of basic epistemic activities, sharing of responsibility for thinking, distribution of the cognitive load among several individuals, airing alternative points of view or alternative solution strategies (and other forms of conflict that can lead to cognitive restructuring), and co-construction of new solutions which take into account differences as well as similarities among the participants. (p. 179)

Conflict resolution education works hand in hand with approaches to education which emphasize social interaction and cooperative and experiential pedagogy. The social skills involved in resolving conflicts provide the foundation for productive learning through social interaction in the classroom.

The social interaction perspective sheds some light on the monarchy versus democracy question we put aside earlier. Classrooms organized around conflict resolution principles, emphasizing cooperative and experiential learning, do tend to be noisier and busier than more structured classrooms. There is social interaction going on here. Traditional pedagogy suggests that learning takes place in a quiet, controlled atmosphere. The social interaction perspective suggests something quite different: learning takes place in the context of social relationships and social interactions. "Controlling" the classroom often ends up stifling children's natural inclination to interact. Rather than reining in this energy, the teacher's role is to use that energy, guiding it towards specific learning objectives. Providing students with conflict resolution skills provides a social framework for the classroom in which interactive learning can take place *without* "losing control." Control, that is, maintaining a safe constructive atmosphere for learning, becomes a function of the students' desire for positive social interactions and learned skill at achieving them.

Conflict Resolution as Institutional and Cultural Change

Of course, we still have not addressed the question of what one does with institutional and social resistance to the sort of comprehensive conflict resolution approach to classroom organization which we have been discussing. There is always resistance to new methods, to change of any kind. This is a particular problem with conflict resolution approaches.

A little bit of conflict resolution is about as effective as a little bit of birth control. We can teach students skills but if we continue to maintain a top-down authoritative approach to classroom discipline, the skills will wither and die for lack of opportunity and lack of motivation to practice them. Instituting a conflict resolution approach in a single classroom can have substantial benefits for the class and the students in it, but will they have an uphill climb if the wider school structure and disciplinary approach is delivering conflicting messages? What will happen to those students' skills in the following year when they scatter to other classes and other classrooms? The successful institutionalization of conflict resolution is not simply a matter of establishing procedures, but is rather a matter of culture change throughout the school and even the surrounding community. Conflict resolution skills cannot be maintained in isolation.

Approaches to culture change in schools include working with teachers, students, administrators and parents. Faculty in-service trainings, presentations at faculty meetings and the creation of a faculty committee for conflict resolution curriculum design often accompany school conflict resolution programs. Presentations at parent meetings and invitations to participate in mediation and other trainings can involve parents and the wider community. The entire student body can be introduced to conflict resolution concepts through school-wide acquaintanceship programs which can involve school assemblies or presentation of conflict resolution mini-workshops in classes. Experience with mediation programs suggests that a critical factor in program success is enthusiastic support from the top administration.

This is not to diminish the efforts of individual teachers. A single lesson which plants the seed of the idea that conflict is something which can be confronted and grappled with can influence the direction of a child's life. The creation of one classroom, one oasis in children's lives, in which conflict is constructively engaged, can provide students with an understanding and appreciation for different ways of being with one another. Culture change is, after all, a process which starts with individuals.

References and Resources

Brownell, Celia. (1989). "Socially shared cognition: The role of social context in the construction of knowledge." In Lucien T. Winegar (Ed.), *Social Interaction and the Development of Children's Understanding*. Norwood, NJ: Ablex Publishing Corporation.

Cheatham, Annie. (1988). *Directory of School Mediation and Conflict Resolution Programs*. Amherst, MA: National Association for Mediation in Education.

Edwards, Carolyn Pope with Ramsey, Patricia G. (1986). *Promoting Social and Moral Development in Young Children*. New York: Teachers College Press.

Garton, Alison F. (1992). *Social Interaction and the Development of Language and Cognition*. Hove, UK: Lawrence Erlbaum Associates Ltd.

Johnson, David W. & Johnson, Roger T. (1991). *Teaching Students to be Peacemakers*. Edina, MN: Interaction Book Company.

Kissner, Robert F. & Beamish, Joanne F. (1987). *Justice Simulations: An Instructional Kit for College Criminology Courses*. New Westminster: Douglas College.

Kreidler, William J. (1984). *Creative Conflict Resolution*. Glenview, IL: Scott Foresman and Company.

Lam, Julie A. (1989). *The Impact of Conflict Resolution Programs on Schools: A Review and Synthesis of the Evidence*. Amherst, MA: National Association for Mediation in Education.

Pilati, David A. (1993). "An agenda for increasing the effectiveness of peer mediation programs." In *The Fourth R* (Vol. 48), Dec. 1993/Jan. 1994. Amherst, MA: National Association for Mediation in Education.

Prutzman, Priscilla, et al. (1988). *The Friendly Classroom for a Small Planet*. Philadelphia: New Society Publishers.

Selman, R. L. (1976). "Social-cognitive understanding." In T. Lickona (Ed.), *Moral Development and Behavior: Theory, Research, and Social Issues*. New York: Holt, Rinehart and Winston.

Winegar, Lucien T. (Ed.). (1989). *Social Interaction and the Development of Children's Understanding*. Norwood, NJ: Ablex Publishing Corporation.

CHAPTER 4
Affirming Democratic Principles in the Classroom

Ruth Yates

An understanding and appreciation of the democratic principles involved in governance can be learned by children through personal classroom experiences. This chapter discusses some theoretical guidelines and practical activities for developing student awareness of the function of rules in society.

Democratic principles are at the foundation of our social, political and legal systems. They should also give shape to social and personal attitudes and values. Not all children are raised with these ideas firmly ingrained in their minds and one of the roles of the school should be to see that democratic concepts are taught and promoted until they become second nature. While teachers cannot control what learnings and attitudes children bring to the classroom, they can create a classroom environment in which positive social attitudes and values are learned and practiced. Unfortunately, policies and rules that affect student behavior are usually set long before the student enters the classroom. They are imposed on students with little reference to the children upon whom they will have the greatest impact. Students are expected to conform to previously established procedures and comply with all the rules in place. To a great extent this is necessary to preserve order and the efficient operation of the school, but those who promote experiential learning suggest that giving students the opportunity to practice the skills of governance by allowing them to play an active role in the creation and enforcement of policies and rules would help them to more effectively live in and contribute to a democratic society.

The extent to which children can participate in the organization and management of their classroom environment will logically depend on the developmental stage of the group and the individual students' capacity to assume responsibility and function in organized groups. Once children become aware of the particular value system that exists in the school, recognize that there are rules and people with the authority to enforce them, they should also begin to understand why. They should be encouraged to ask questions about the system and the rules and be given the means to determine when an authority figure is legitimate and should be obeyed. Lessons are not the best way to teach children these concepts. Students must experience how social organizations function and much of this can be achieved within the school.

Children should develop pro-social attitudes and practice social skills sooner than it has been the tradition to introduce them in the curriculum. Too often schools and classrooms have been places where children are greeted with a seemingly endless array of rules, that they only discover exist when they break them, that have no meaning for them and that are set by someone who inexplicably has great power over them. The primary objective of schools to teach the curriculum then justifies the imposition of external control with little thought in these early grades to teaching the skills of self-determination and self-governance. The need to socialize only becomes apparent when hitherto compliant children suddenly begin to act out, to resist authority and to attempt to create their own agenda for school. By the sixth or seventh grades, if children have not already gained an appreciation of personal, group and societal values, and how they interrelate, they begin to sense that the system has managed to deprive them of their freedom and personal rights and that the only way to retrieve them is to fight the system. If they learn early that this new group to which they have been introduced is there to serve, help and train them and that without it many good things in life would not be possible, they will have a desire to contribute positively to the group, not only in their own self-interest but also in the interest of others within the group.

They should have a right to enjoy the benefits of being part of a group, and that includes the right not to be hurt or interfered with. They should gain some sense of power over themselves and their circumstances and recognize that they have a responsibility to contribute to the harmony and successes of the group and often therein lies their own capacity to achieve. They need to understand that social living demands that people recognize, acknowledge, cooperate and participate in the group. Teachers can enhance the possibility of children gaining group values while still enabling them to recognize and exercise the independent thinking and personal integrity necessary to prevent individuals from being misled by the inappropriate use of authority or peer pressure.

Background Considerations

Before looking at how a democratic classroom should be set up, let's look at some of the background factors that contribute to the need for practical lessons in democratic living. Children come to school and into the classroom with widely different conceptions of right and wrong and of what is appropriate or improper behavior. Some are confident, independent and assertive, others shy, insecure and reticent.

The fortunate ones have stable, confident parents who raise them in an atmosphere of acceptance and support for the growing up they have to do. Their behavior at school tends to mirror that stability.... The unfortunate ones live in emotionally and physically unstable situations almost from birth. Their behavior, too, mirrors what they have learned. (Newman, 1993, p. 5)

Some come from troubled homes where violence and abuse are a way of life; some through poverty lack the basic necessities of healthful life, others who are well-provided for come from homes where adults are away much of the time. The expectations of the school are great.

For many children, school is the safest place in their world; it is the place where adults set out deliberately to know and care about them, work with them, show them compassion, and demonstrate responsibility. Teachers may not be able to change the circumstances these children face outside the school building, but they can help to ensure that the time they spend in school is safe and good. (Newman, 1993, p. 5)

What the school can offer that may help children from both troubled and secure home environments is consistency, predictability and models of appropriate adult social behavior that may be lacking in their family lives. It should also be a warm and inviting place that is attractive and welcoming to children. Further, it should be a place where children's individual strengths are discovered and developed and where their vulnerabilities are acknowledged but are compensated for and the assistance provided that is necessary to help them overcome some of the personal problems that they face. Dreeben contends that the

Emotions aroused in schooling derive from events in which the pupils' sense of self-respect is either supported or threatened. ... this influences the pupils in deciding whether or not they will find their early experiences at school enjoyable enough to act according to the standards governing school activities. (Dreeben, 1968, p. 135)

Given the tools and skills to work with, the opportunity to apply them in school and encouragement to adopt them in their personal lives, children, who are naturally resilient, can become strong, resourceful and self-confident people who will become contributing members of their own communities and break the cycles of neglect and abuse that may have been factors in their early lives.

A recent task force report on violence in the schools suggests that there is as much concern with violence and aggression among the youngest students as there is with violence among older students. Among the operating principles of the report is the statement that the panel preferred to think in terms of violence prevention.

> While we recognize the importance of strong interventions for dealing with violent incidents, we believe that a focus on violence prevention, particularly with young children, through a variety of means, holds greater promise for addressing the problem.

There is also the acknowledgement that

> Schools are not isolated; they are part of the community and reflect the society around them . . . and violence is not just a school problem, and that solutions, as well, will involve the broader community. (British Columbia Teachers' Federation, 1994, p. 4)

The task force identified a number of trends that are of particular concern among younger-aged children.

> Teachers have noticed aggressive behavior among children as young as five – incidents such as biting, kicking, or punching teachers and other children, and using extremely violent language. . . . Some teachers are noticing that children resort to violence to resolve conflict more quickly than in the past. . . . There seems to be an increasing level of challenge to authority and to authority figures, including teachers, principals, and police. Teachers and parents have reported that young people have less fear about the consequences of their actions. (British Columbia Teachers' Federation, 1994, p. 6)

These are only some of the negative symptoms being manifested among schoolchildren. Others are fear, alienation, insecurity, helplessness, frustration, lethargy and indifference, the sense that there is no point in applying oneself to schoolwork, because it isn't going to make a difference in the long run. These feelings too often lead to withdrawal from the group, defiance of authority and finally dropping out of school altogether. What is required, as the Task Force suggests, is a "new community where violence is unlikely to occur" (p. 4).

Many early schooling experiences give ambiguous messages to children about which aspects of their personhood are acceptable and which are not. Children are praised for controlling their emotions and for being quiet and compliant and they are reprimanded for talking and moving out of turn. They are encouraged to stand on their own, be resourceful and independent, but are treated as just one of a group which must be controlled. What they should experience in their first classrooms is a sense of safety, comfort and friendship, and opportunities and stimuli to learn and socialize. This is found when the children have some meaningful input into how their time is organized and where there is a group of other children with whom they are encouraged to forge close associations within a framework in which positive interrelations are fostered.

Among the comprehensive plans listed by the Task Force to combat the problems of violence in the schools is one calling for "social skills programs taught to all students from school entry to grade 12." A more effective recommendation might be stated as follows "positive social attitudes and skills be *learned and practiced* by all students from school entry to grade 12." Socializing concepts, moral principles and positive social attitudes and skills can be relayed to young children best, not through structured curricular teaching, but through daily experiences in the classroom.

Children become aware through the course of daily living that there are people in their lives who have authority over them. Very early they develop the attitudes towards authority that they will carry with them for the rest of their lives. Attitudes are based on their experiences with authority figures. A recent study conducted in the United States by Tom Tyler suggests very strongly that adults' willingness to comply with laws depends largely on their perceptions of how fairly they were treated by people who had authority over them when they were young (Tyler, 1990, pp. 94-112). While these initial perceptions are acquired in the home, the next most influential place is the school, and it seems especially to be the case for those who have had negative experiences with authority, either through absence, abuse or over-exertion at home, that are reinforced in the school. That is, children who do not have adequately developed social skills when they come to school inevitably call upon their heads the full force of authority from the principal, their teachers and even their classmates. Having had little or no experience with the appropriate role of authority, their aggregate experiences make them unwilling to comply with its dictates as they grow. What they need is to come to an understanding of how people get their authority, what purpose it serves and when it is being used legitimately.

Children also experience and are required to live by many rules which have a seemingly unlimited number of sources and functions. Rules, without reasons to support them, become unbearable and eventually meaningless. What children can learn though experiences in the classroom is why rules are necessary, how they are made, and when and how they can be changed. They may also feel first-hand what rights they have as individuals and why it is important to respect the rights of others. They can come to know that social living depends on every person accepting responsibility for their own actions and cooperating with and helping others to understand and accept their responsibilities. They can begin to make links between what happens in their classrooms and schools and what happens in the larger community, and thereby feel more secure and comfortable in it.

> Children ought to have an opportunity to make rules, study them, amend them, and live by them. They ought to analyze why a move from the classroom to a ball diamond changes the "rules" and the expectations about noise and movement. They are able very early to understand the system of "rules" and can be helped to view that system in terms of the need for order and, therefore, justice. (Falkenstein and Anderson, 1980, p. 229)

School Governance

Schools can be structured in such a way that the children can have freedom of action and decision in many ways. In order to learn responsibility for their decisions and actions, they need to be given the opportunity to exercise them. There are some decisions that affect the entire school population that students can have some input into. These might include what activities are available during the recess period or the organization and supervision of lunch break and after-school sports. Within the classroom children can help schedule academic work, outdoor play, field trips and social activities. It is usually not practical or advisable to have standing school-wide student committees at the elementary level. The time-frame is too long for most young children, the opportunity to represent and lead can be made available to only a few children, and unless there are real problems for the committee to work on, they may feel that their time spent in committee meetings is pointless. A more effective approach might be to ask for students to help solve problems when they come up.

Every school ought to face a number of problems throughout the year or it suggests that the school is too tightly structured and controlled by administrators and/or teachers for optimal social learning to occur (Falkenstein, p. 139). Some of the problems that are of general concern to the school population – vandalism, racism, formation of gangs, unsafe situations developing in the playground or common areas of the school, or how to spend funds that children have helped to raise, etc. – would be appropriate reasons to call a teacher and student committee together to try to help find a solution. In such instances representatives could be selected from each class to meet with school administrators and teachers to articulate and discuss the problem. Committee members could then meet with the children in their classrooms and return with suggestions, which could be discussed and adopted by the group. New rules could be created and reasons developed for them. Each representative could then take the outcome of the committee's discussion back to their own class-room and inform their peers of the new rules and help in the supervision of the rules and reporting back on whether or not the problem is solved by the action taken. In this manner children have the opportunity to work on a real problem in a meaningful way and to see the immediate effects of their taking concrete action. Trying out new rules promotes recognition that rules and laws are established to solve problems and that they can be changed when the need arises.

A spirit of participation and cooperation among all the members of the school community can do more to enhance feelings of self-worth, confidence, personal security, belonging and institutional pride than any top-down style of school admin-istration. The attitudes and practices of adults in the school shape the feelings and expectations of children in this, their first formal institution, and prepare them for their participation in society.

Learning related to cooperation, respect for individuals, property and authority, fairness, the need for rules, and responsibility can and should be taught in schools, and ultimately forms the foundations upon which democratic governance rests. Such concepts are best taught when based on the direct experiences of children and when the schools themselves provide models who constantly function in terms of these values. (Falkenstein, p. 141)

Class Governance

A school organization that is mirrored in the classroom further enhances the success of the school community and gives children the opportunity to practice leadership skills. A teacher who wants to encourage children to govern their own behavior will demonstrate attitudes and skills that include a willingness to be aware of and feel a sense of responsibility for all the children in the school. A teacher should always be willing to give a reason for requiring certain behaviors as this shows respect for the children and recognizes their need and ability to understand. A teacher must value and live by principles of fairness and equality and demonstrate a respectful cooperation in her associations with other adults in the school community. Among the skills of an effective teacher will be to model desirable behaviors and to lead discussions in which children are given the opportunity to express and test their ideas, opinions and feelings. A teacher must be able to guide rule- and decision-making processes without dominating the exercise and show by verbal responses that the child's sincere contributions are respected and valued. Another essential skill is to do much of this with a sense of humor along with the capacity to lighten the workload and charm children into desirable behaviors (Falkenstein, pp. 140-141).

What follows is a step-by-step plan for organizing a class and is applicable to any grade level in elementary school. The earlier such plans are incorporated, the greater the level of participation. As the children develop and become experienced in using leadership, cooperation and conflict management techniques, the less need there will be for external controls being exercised by school staff. The description of the method includes a number of suggestions that may be helpful in implementing the program in your classroom.

Step 1 – Creating a Feeling of Equality

Equality is a difficult principle to establish in family life where a natural hierarchy determines the amount of power a family member has. The classroom is the first real opportunity to help a child recognize that he or she shares equally in the rights, rewards and responsibilities of the group, but that each of those are incumbent on every member of the group acknowledging the rights of every other.

> Everyone has equal value as a person; everyone's feelings are important and everyone has the right to express how they are feeling and has the right to be respected for who they are.

For younger children, learning to sing as a group is an exercise that requires everyone to contribute and there are many popular children's songs that speak of sharing, respecting and expressing feelings. The outcome of many of the games children play in which everyone is included can provide opportunities to discuss the benefits of inclusion, participation and cooperation. Extra effort should be made at the beginning of the year to include those children who, for whatever reason, are reluctant to join in. Careful assignment of buddies whose personalities and temperaments balance one another is a beneficial exercise.

Step 2 – Establishing a Sense of Individuality

Devise a "getting to know you" style game that acknowledges each child for bringing something special and unique to the classroom and emphasizes that differences are important to make the class balanced and complete. Draw analogies from the game to the classroom. For example, each child tells something about him or herself or their family, place of origin or what they like to do, and the teacher or fellow students point out a personal quality, skill or strength that comes from that fact. ("I have four brothers and sisters" – that would make you patient, or "I come from Hong Kong" – you've seen a part of the world that we haven't, or "I play street hockey" – you know how to be part of a team.)

Personal differences make a group more interesting and fun. Find positive qualities that can be developed out of characteristics that may at first seem distracting or annoying. For example, a hyperactive child has enough energy to keep us all involved in a project. A tearful child reminds us when we have to be more sensitive or inclusive.

Step 3 – Identifying the Purpose of School

The children are asked what they would like to gain from coming to school and being in this classroom. Point out that we all have goals and we all want to achieve them and be someone special. The discussion might follow upon the these kinds of questions and observations. Can we do this all by ourselves? That's why we live in family groups and have classroom groups in school. We help each other achieve our goals. Everyone in this class can contribute something to help another student be successful. What do you think that might be? Maybe you know something another student doesn't know. Perhaps you have something another needs. Perhaps if I stop what I'm doing (i.e., talking or taking over) another person and our group can be more successful. What can you do to make this classroom a happy place for someone else? [I can help, I can show, I can teach, I can be kind, I can encourage, I can listen. I won't intimidate, or hurt or make fun of other children.] If people treat you with kindness and respect, how does it make you feel?

Step 4 – Establishing Classroom Rules

Opening discussion: What rules should everyone be required to obey? [The ones that keep us safe.] Why are they important? [So everyone knows how to act and what to expect of others.] What should we do if someone breaks a rule? [Help them know that breaking rules hurts someone. Understand what it feels like to be hurt.] Is it important to have consequences?

Create a set of general class rules and the consequences for breaking them. This should be a group effort. The teacher asks for ideas for rules and writes them on the blackboard (or provides illustrations of them for non-readers). Once everyone's ideas have been recorded, the children are asked which of the rules is most important and should come first. Distinguish for them between legal rules – these are rules that protect us and our belongings from being hurt by others, and social rules – rules that make the classroom a happy, comfortable place for everyone. Rules are then listed in the priority suggested by the students. Then select up to seven that they consider the most important and have them written on a permanent chart for display in a prominent place in the classroom.

Rules that should be included are ones that affect:

1. Individual Rights

Everyone has the right not to be touched or harmed by someone else. Every person has the right to feel comfortable, happy and secure. They have a right to private space and a right to share common space. They have a right to be different, to have different ideas and opinions. And they have a right to express those ideas unless they hurt someone else and make them uncomfortable, unhappy and insecure.

2. General School Rules

The teacher may have to point out some school rules that are already in place and that children must obey.

3. Social Rules

These are optional – at the discretion of students and the teacher. They may include such rules as:

✎ Take turns using school supplies and equipment

✎ Treat others with consideration and respect

✐ No gum chewing, etc.

Obtaining a Commitment to Live by the Class Rules

Responsibility to the Group – What happens if any of these rules are broken? What happens if we don't have any rules? Obtain a commitment from each student to live by the rules by asking the following question: Does everyone agree to live by the rules that the class has established? It is a good idea to insure this either by raising their hands or for older children to produce a written commitment that could read, I, _____, agree to live by the classroom rules while I am in school.

Step 5 – Making the Rules Work

Ask students for suggestions as to what should be the consequence for breaking each of the class rules. Teachers should qualify each response to be sure students understand that the consequence should fit the offense and that they are not excessively harsh. Explain or ask children to suggest what punishment is for – to help a person understand that someone suffers when a rule is broken and when one person is hurt everyone is injured, to discourage people from hurting others, to help everyone feel safe and happy in the classroom. Who should be responsible for carrying out the punishment? Usually it is the group that has been hurt by the offending action. Explain the difference between revenge – getting back at a person for hurting you – and suffering consequences for your action. Only the affected group, thinking and acting together, should have the right to administer consequences. Only rarely should a teacher be responsible for punishing offenders. This is the responsibility of the group that makes the rules.

Normally, the appropriate consequence for breaking classroom rules would be the withdrawal of privileges. This suggests that there ought to be enough things happening in the class that the children really enjoy doing that removal of those opportunities would be enough to discourage them from breaking agreed-upon rules. The class should help to establish which rules are so important that only the teacher and or the principal should be involved in dealing with the offense. Because it would not be very efficient for everyone to be involved every time someone breaks a rule, a conflict committee made up of the teacher and group leaders will have the responsibility of dealing with all but the most and least serious infractions. Teachers should help children distinguish between serious and minor problems and to understand how the problem changes when it moves from being a single occurrence to a repeated occurrence. The composition of this committee is described under "Group Organizations."

Step 6 – How Do Rules Work in the Community?

Explain that classroom rules are just like the rules that govern our neighborhoods, towns and country. Everyone is subject to many rules and everyone has a responsibility to know what they are and to obey them. If we don't know all the rules, there are a few questions we can ask ourselves if we are wondering whether there is a rule about something we want to do. Is it safe? Will it hurt someone or damage something? Is it fair? Would I be upset if someone did it to me or to my things?

Our country is too big to have just one person who makes the rules and enforces them and so the country is divided up into a lot of smaller groups of people who each have responsibility for looking after the people in their own group. These groups are called provinces, towns and neighborhoods. The leaders appointed or elected by each group work together to make sure that their group is living up to the expectations of the larger community or nation groups.

Point out to students that in order for a group to be effective it mustn't be too big and probably 30-32 students in a class is too many for a workable group, as they may have noticed when everyone was trying to contribute to the rule-making process. Once everyone has agreed on the big rules (the ones that affect everyone in the class), then the day-to-day operation of the class can best be managed in smaller groups.

Step 7 – Organizing the Class

Divide the class into four groups of 6-8 students each. (The teacher should select students for these groups ensuring that there is an equitable mix of boys and girls, ethnic groups and strong and weak students. It is best to resist pressure from students to be in the same group as their friends. Explain that you are trying to widen their circle of friends.) The groups will elect a group leader, by first recognizing two nominees and then having the members cast a secret ballot to elect a leader. The second nominee can become an assistant to the leader and substitute if the leader is away. Group leaders function for one month and each student should have the opportunity to be a group leader during the school year. At the end of each month the group leader rotates into one of the other groups (their choice or by drawing lots). This means that each student will participate in two different groups during the year. The group is then given a list of responsibilities and it is the group leader's job to see that they are accomplished and everyone is having their needs met and is contributing to the success of the group.

It is preferable that the group members be physically close to one another in the classroom. This can be accomplished by their using one large table or by grouping desks together. This facilitates the students working collaboratively on many learning projects throughout the year.

Groups should have some degree of autonomy. They should be responsible for their area of the classroom, how it is organized, decorated, kept clean and tidy. They may name the group by consensus, with the teacher able to veto any names that are derogatory or overly competitive. Anytime a teacher's right to veto is used, the teacher should explain why and guidance should be given as to a more appropriate course of action.

The teacher presents each group with a list of individual and group responsibilities and the group conducts a discussion as to how the responsibilities will be carried out, delegated and accounted for.

This list may include the following:

Academic Work

- Organizing, storing and maintaining personal belongings and school supplies
- Distributing work assignments and collecting completed work
- Maintaining assignment charts
- Organizing the group to work on cooperative projects
- Setting up peer tutoring and/or a buddy system

Social Activities

- Group solves minor rule infractions
- Group leaders form a conflict committee with teacher at its head to deal with more serious rule infractions. Conflict committee meets when necessary or once a week to review the rules and make changes
- Plan and organize class social activities or special projects for periods devoted to music, art and P.E.

[One hour each week, a Friday afternoon perhaps, may be devoted to giving one of the groups an opportunity to develop and present an enrichment activity in the form of a story drama, role play, mock trial or other fun activity for the rest of the class. These may be coordinated with special holidays throughout the year. Each group would have the opportunity to conduct this activity once a month and planning and preparation for the event would be the focus of their collaborative efforts. Direction and assistance should be given by teacher and may include the kinds of activities suggested in other chapters of this text.]

Housekeeping Duties

- The teacher could use the groups to accomplish many of the regular housekeeping activities required in the classroom. If the expectations are clear, the groups can assume responsibility for them and assign them to members of the group. Older children can determine what needs to be done and assign responsibility.

Failure to meet group expectations ought to have a consequence attached that the group can monitor and apply. Groups that have learned to work cooperatively are ideally positioned to help each other with academic tasks such as proof-reading, editing and correcting, reading and spelling practice, arithmetic drills. The idea is to encourage the children to help and teach one another and share in the responsibility of learning. Groups can be evaluated on how effectively they work together, how few rule infractions there are and how well they learn the material as a group. Part of their grade can be based on how well the group performs relative to the other groups. Care should be taken not to develop too strong a competitive spirit between groups in the classroom.

Group leaders need to be given instruction on how to manage the group and a brief meeting should be held for new group leaders at the beginning of each month. They should be given a system for taking notes of decisions made so there is no dispute later, delegating responsibilities and learn how to get an accounting of things accomplished. They should get the children to help draft a report at the end of each week to report to the teachers as to their progress and accomplishments. The format may be very simple for younger grades, amounting to stickers on a prepared chart, and more complex for older grades, requiring them to submit a brief written report compiled by group members. These reports can become part of student-led parent/teacher conferences which may be part of the evaluation process.

Much of this effort can be facilitated by helping the groups to become independently-functioning units where the students clearly understand the teacher's expectations and are given the means and opportunity to accomplish their assigned responsibilities. The group scheme suggested in the chapter could be used to facilitate classroom organization and regular group assignments. Opportunities should be provided for children to work in other groups constituted for other purposes or projects so that they can interact with other children throughout the year. This may be accomplished by assigning the children in each group a number between one and eight and on occasion calling all the children with the same number to work in a group for a special project and mixing the numbers each time.

Conflict Committee

All children in the class will have the opportunity to serve on the class Conflict Committee for one month of the year as part of their leadership rotation and so each will have an opportunity to learn and practice mediation and conflict resolution skills. The leaders' meeting held at the beginning of the month should include a session led by the teacher providing instruction on how to identify and mediate in conflict situations. Basic conflict resolution skills should include the following:

Being Aware

Members of the Conflict Committee should be watchful and recognize early signs of problems, such as:

✏ a child calling another names or threatening

- a child being excluded from games
- games that become too boisterous or children acting aggressively towards one another

Receiving a report

When an incident takes place and a committee member becomes aware of it, he or she should approach the children involved and ask others to disperse.

Intervention strategies:

- Identify oneself as a member of the Conflict Committee
- Offer to mediate
  - Ask each of children involved what the problem is
  - Ask who is responsible for the problem
  - Ask how this problem can be solved
  - If the parties agree to the solution, then the matter is concluded and no report may be needed.

The mediator should not get involved in the conflict or allow the situation to become a shouting match between the parties. If the mediator cannot help in the situation, an adult should be called in but the adult's role should be as an aid to the student mediator and to reinforce their strategy. Sometimes it is best to separate the parties, allow for some cooling-off time and indicate that they will be required to report to a class Conflict Committee hearing which should be conducted a soon as possible after the incident if it is serious.

Conflict Committee Guidelines

The student who attempted the initial mediation should describe the situation to the Conflict Committee when it meets. The children involved in the dispute should then be given an opportunity to explain their positions and why there has been no resolution to the problem. If it is clear that one child is responsible, that should be acknowledged by the committee and that child should be asked what an appropriate consequence would be. If it is agreeable to the Conflict Committee, arrangements should be made for the child to report on the consequence being accomplished. A record should be kept of the incident and when the same child is required to come before the committee for the same or similar offenses for a third time, the teacher should become involved in the process to arrange for more serious consequences. Disciplinary action should be noted and then removed when the offender has satisfactorily modified his or her behavior or there have been no repeat offenses within the month. It helps for the teacher to be seen treating an offending child with warmth and affection and encourages other children to do likewise and to respond positively to disciplinary action when it is necessary.

Teacher Preparation and Evaluation

The teacher should prepare wall charts for each group to record progress in both academic and social areas. The group recorder will be given instructions on how to keep the charts up to date and the completed chart will be part of a month-end group report. Month-end reports should include completed charts, a statement from each child about what they liked or didn't like about being part of the group, a de-briefing report and evaluation of group week-end activity, an assessment of general deportment of the group and their area.

Teachers may give students as much flexibility in completing assignments as seems appropriate. Privileges may be extended to students completing assignments in an efficient and satisfactory manner. Privileges may include the opportunity to visit the library, play quiet board games, work on arts and crafts projects or do computer work. If the entire group successfully completes the assigned work and other expectations in a given week, group privileges may be extended which may include outdoor play time or a field trip activity or a special lunch. These incentives should be made known to the groups at the beginning of the year.

The teacher's role in facilitating group work will involve some pre-class preparation which might include decisions on how large the groups will be and the assignment of group members. Arranging the room and dividing up learning materials will also be part of the preparation process. When the groups have been established it is important to constantly encourage the children to work together and to cooperate in accomplishing their group and individual assignments. This process is facilitated by suggesting goals for the group, structuring ways of accounting for progress, explaining what is expected and specifying desired behaviors. The next step is to monitor group activity and provide task assistance when necessary. The teacher also brings closure to group sessions and helps groups to move on to the next lesson or activity. The on-going evaluation of the quantity and quality of students' learning, and also assessing group function, is an important part of the process and may be facilitated by conducting a group conference at the end of each month. The group conference may include parents, giving children the opportunity to review their work and share their group experiences with their parents.

What follows are guidelines that the teacher might use to help students develop class rules and work in groups. Also included are directions for the creation and function of a conflict committee.

Teacher Guidelines for Organizing a Democratic Classroom

Suggested Class Rules

- No hitting or annoying
- No interfering, damaging or destroying school or other people's property
- No swearing or name calling
- No intimidating (taunting, threatening or harassing)
  optional: (social rules – for the comfort and enjoyment of all members of the class)
- No spitting, gum chewing, eating, hat wearing, running, interrupting in class

Incorporating School Rules

- Obtain approval from class members
- Get commitments from class members
- Students understand consequences of failing to obey rules

Group Guidelines

Composition

- Composed of up to eight students and constituted for a full school year – leaders are rotated monthly.
- When the group convenes at the beginning of a month, they nominate two possible leaders. Each group member casts one vote for their choice of leader.
- The student nominated and elected by the group serves as leader for only one month of year and then moves to a new group when the month's leadership period ends.
- Assistant leader – the 2nd nominee may become recorder for the group and fills in when leader is absent.
- Each group member assumes an area of responsibility for the month. (These vary with classroom organization, but may include housekeeping tasks, collecting assignments, assisting teacher, maintaining group charts, reporting progress.)

Leader's Responsibilities

- Attend leader training with teacher at beginning of month session
- Conduct group meeting once a week (time allowed can vary, depending on need, from 15 to 30 minutes)

- Assign individual responsibilities

- Assign peer tutors

- Organize group's monthly activity session

- Supervise and assist in completion of month-end report

- Participate on Conflict Committee

    - Receive reports of rule infractions by group members

    - Schedule Conflict Committee hearing when required

    - Attend scheduled Conflict Committee meetings

Conflict Committee Guidelines

A group leader receiving a report of a rule infraction

- attempts to mediate

- reports to teacher, and, if it is deemed necessary,

- will call a meeting of the Conflict Committee comprising the teacher and group leaders.

Offending student(s) will be called before the committee and asked the following questions:

1. What is the problem?

2. Whose problem is this?

3. What do you want to have happen?

4. What alternatives can you accept?

- Conflict committee in the presence of offender briefly brainstorms possible solutions

- Conflict committee and offenders come to agreement on specific action to be taken.

- One committee member assumes responsibility for following up to see that the problem has been satisfactorily resolved.

References and Resources

British Columbia Teachers Federation. (1994). *Report of the Task Force on Violence in the Schools*. Vancouver, B.C.

Carter, Margaret. (1980). "Law and values in American society." In L. Falkenstein and C. Anderson (Eds.), *Daring to Dream: Law and the Humanities for Elementary Schools.* Chicago, IL: American Bar Association Special Committee on Youth Education for Citizenship.

Dreeben, H. (1968). *On What is Learned in School.* Reading, MA: Addison-Wesley.

Falkenstein, Lynda Carl & Anderson, Charlotte C. (Eds.). (1980). *Daring to Dream: Law and the Humanities for Elementary Schools.* Chicago, IL: American Bar Association Special Committee on Youth Education for Citizenship.

Newman, Fran. (1993). *Children in Crisis.* Toronto: Scholastic.

Tyler, Tom R. (1990). *Why People Obey the Law.* New Haven, CT: Yale University Press.

CHAPTER 5
Looking at Law Through Story Drama

Heather Gascoigne

Children love a good story and when they are given the opportunity to participate in the story, they not only come to know but also feel what the characters experience. Story drama allows them to gain a sense of the purpose and need for laws.

Among the many ways that children can come to know something about the law and how it works is by "living" it. Although we are not always aware of it, the law affects almost every aspect of human activity. It defines most of our relationships, places limits on our behavior, protects us from those who do not obey the law and grants us a remedy when we have been harmed by someone's illegal act. We cannot walk down the street, get on a bus, join a club, purchase a product or watch a movie without being affected by a law. It is difficult to imagine all of the possible scenarios that students might find themselves in and even more difficult to reproduce them in the classroom. But doing so would give children a chance to decide before they were faced with a situation how they might handle it, what effect their decision would have on others and how it would be interpreted by those charged with enforcing the law. Simulation exercises help children identify problems, practice decision-making skills and appreciate the consequences of their actions. One of the best ways to engage young children in a simulated activity is to entice them into it with a story.

Using Drama as a Teaching Technique

My experience in elementary classrooms has confirmed that story drama enables students to explore a variety of subject areas, gain new understandings and experience a shift in attitudes. Dramatic activity provides the opportunity to learn from "within" the experience, rather than simply studying "about" something. It allows children to assess a situation, work cooperatively together to solve a problem, relate the experiences of others to their own lives and reflect on what they have learned. One of the responsibilities of a teacher is to help students make connections between the knowledge and skills they already possess and the experiences of others. As participants in a dramatic activity assume the identity of another they can begin to identify with a different place and time, see things from another perspective and gain new understandings from the experience.

I am not talking about drama for its own sake – the kind which is a performance for others. Dorothy Heathcote reiterates that "The difference between theatre and classroom drama is that in theatre every thing is contrived so that the audience gets the kicks. In the classroom, the participants get the kicks" (1979, p. 147). There is no audience. Everyone in the classroom is involved. Classroom drama provides the opportunity to "take part" in the experience and should not be confused with "acting out" a role. A human dilemma derived from a story and presented through drama allows role-takers to think from within an experience, to examine and solve a problem as though it were their own. The situation must be powerful enough to engage participants emotionally so they are committed to think through the problem, examine the alternatives and make new choices. Experiencing other perspectives is essential to changing attitudes and developing new understandings. Heathcote is committed "to helping students get the idea that drama is about what's underneath the action . . . getting to the universal. Once they have had that experience, they'll know it forever" (p. 36).

Starting with Stories

Story drama is not simply the "acting out" of stories. It is using literature as the "jumping off" point to initiate the drama experience. "Drama becomes a tool for the exploration of the ideas, relationships, and language of the story. . . . By joining story and drama, children can combine an interest in the lives of story characters with an inner exploration of themselves and their own struggles for control over their lives" (Barton and Booth, 1990, p. 136). Through drama, stories can liberate childrens' imaginations, develop thinking skills and improve their capacity to express themselves orally, in writing and in art. Exploring and extending a story through drama helps children find and reflect on new levels of meaning. Drama can function across the curriculum, integrating many different subject areas.

Experiencing stories helps children to recognize their place in society, acquire the skills to function in the community and create a desire to make a contribution to its well-being. Carole Tarlington has worked with children for many years, using the elements of drama in education. In her article, "Role Drama: A Strategy which Promotes Thinking," she points out that drama is more that just an expressive medium. She believes that the process is a cognitive one in which students, "face issues, examine attitudes, grasp concepts, solve problems, research, observe, listen critically, make judgments, reflect, extend language, cooperate with others, and learn the content of the subject being explored" (1982, p. 1). My experience using drama within the context of children's literature has proven to be the most effective and successful teaching strategy for helping children know and understand how laws are created, how they work and why they are necessary.

A teacher who uses stories as the base for drama activities must build up a repertoire of stories from which to draw. Included at the end of this chapter is an annotated list of stories I have used to enhance law-related learnings in my classes. However, the story drama strategy can be used in a multitude of educational contexts.

> Teaching and learning never change without a special kind of imaginative act, which all the curriculum guides in the world cannot render unnecessary. You may be inspired to turn your classroom into one where stories flow and become a major means of learning and developing linguistic powers. But then, you need to translate your enthusiasm into day-to-day practices. How will you make your first move[?] How do you learn to extend your use of stories[?] Where will you find them? How, in a phrase, do your principles undergo that amazing metamorphosis into everyday encounters[?] Only by your own imaginative weighing of your students . . . and yourself. You must trust your own inventiveness. (Barton & Booth, 1990, p. 91)

How to Begin

I would like to demonstrate the process by recounting my experiences with a grade two class as we studied a unit about the community in Social Studies. Before telling the class the story, I spent a number of periods preparing them to take part in role-playing activities. These exercises are confidence builders which encourage individual as well as group involvement. There are a number of drama books which present engaging confidence-building activities. Two of my favorites are *Offstage: Elementary Education Through Drama* (1982) by Carole Tarlington and Patrick Verriour (Oxford University Press) and *The Incredible Indoor Games Book* (1982) by Bob Gregson (Fearon Teacher Aids). Pre-drama activities give students practice in stretching their imaginations and communicating their feelings and ideas. As such activities are undertaken throughout the year, a sense of trust builds within the group as both the teacher and children see and relate to each other in a number of different roles.

Part of the pre-activity planning includes the development of learning outcomes. These may be modified or added as the activity progresses, but a teacher must have a clear sense of what kind of story and dramatic experiences will lead students to a greater level of understanding of the concepts that are to be taught. In the unit about the Community for instance, it was important that children understand where they belong in the structure of the community, that they gain a sense of the responsibilities of parents, families, neighbors, community workers and elected leaders. Children need to know the laws and rules that affect them, how they came to be and why and how they are enforced. They need to understand that everyone must contribute to the well-being of the community and that everyone has the right to feel safe and comfortable in their community. These may be difficult concepts for young people to appreciate on an abstract level, but take on real meaning when children assume roles of citizens in a story-book community.

In spite of the need for learning outcomes, it is important to allow the participants to give direction and impetus to the story drama. Pre-planning which outlines the framework and context for the story is necessary, but the resolution of the story dilemma must develop from the decisions and actions of the characters. The teacher initiates the drama, but must not lead the children to a solution that has been pre-determined. Children must be allowed to work out the choices they have made and to take responsibility for their decisions. The role of the teacher is to challenge the children to refine and reflect on their choices. In fact reflection on the consequences of those decisions is a crucial part of the debriefing process which should follow each day's scenario and which may have some impact on how the storyline continues but should not prescribe it.

By assuming a role as a character in the drama the teacher demonstrates that she is also willing to take a risk and can invite the children to share in that risk. The teacher 'in role' can assist the students to broaden and deepen their dramatic experience. "This deepening of the level of the drama is the one thing classes cannot manage without a teacher. The teacher can move the class from a general idea to a dramatic focus and then to a universal" (Wagner, 1979, p. 59). By helping students to identify with the drama and reflect on the implications of their choices, by not allowing an easy way out, a teacher can make every action significant. One of the great challenges is to slow the pace so that the actors can analyze what has happened and apply what they've learned not only to the rest of the story drama but transfer to their own life experiences.

The ultimate goal is to empower the students to take responsibility for the direction of the drama. Accepting the suggestions of the students makes it more likely that they will commit themselves to the experience not only on a physical level, but also on a cognitive and affective level. It is important to allow each child to bring something personal to the role he/she is developing. Dorothy Heathcote calls this "starting from within." "As a child sees the relationship between one experience and others which are like it in some important respect, the experience is illuminated by the light of the comparison and a way into a new situation is provided" (1979, p. 52).

And finally, it is important to allow time for the participants to find their way into the dramatic experience. We all need time to establish our identity and role. Build in activities and discussions which will make this possible. Once the participants identify with their characters in the drama, true belief and committal to the process will happen and the combined energy of the group experience will be released which will enable that moment of awareness when true learning can take place. I know of no other method of teaching which has the power to help students expand their understanding of themselves and others from the "inside out." Remember, we are not "making plays" for others, but burnishing our experience through participation in a process which will enable a change of understanding and a deepening of knowledge.

Story Drama Unit – The Pied Piper

I chose the story of the "Pied Piper" because it offered the opportunity to explore both social and legal issues. The people of Hamlin lost their children because the elected officials breached a contract with the Pied Piper. They had agreed to pay 1200 guilders to the Piper to rid their town of rats. When he did so they refused to pay him the amount agreed upon. In order to teach them a lesson, the Pied Piper led the town's children away by playing a magical tune on his pipe and refused to return them until he got full payment for his work. The dilemma for the townspeople was how to get their children back.

With the students gathered together on the story rug, I proceeded to tell a version of this well-known story. Upon finishing, I closed the book, stood up and started pacing the room as an elderly person. I explained that I had called them together for an emergency meeting of the townspeople. I, their Mayor, had a serious problem to discuss with them. I knew they were angry with me. I had received their petition and watched their march to the steps of the town hall. I admitted they had a right to be angry with me because it was my decision not to honor our bargain with the Pied Piper and as a consequence, our children were gone. I asked for their understanding and forgiveness, and requested that they let me stay on as their Mayor to help solve the problem.

My "act" started a buzz of talk among the students. They immediately assumed the roles of distraught parents. One townsperson finally announced that they should let me try, as "everyone deserves a second chance." I was very impressed with their generosity. They knew I had not fulfilled my responsibilities as their Mayor, yet they seemed to recognize that they also had a certain responsibility because they had elected me. We discussed our unhappiness at the loss of our children. This provided an opportunity for the students to build belief into their roles. They were able to "see" what our town looked like, to explain what our role was in the community and to share our grief. I wanted the students to experience being part of a community which depended on each other.

One child said he owned the candy store. He hadn't made any money since the children disappeared. Another owned a toy store. No one was buying toys anymore. I told them that I knew this was all my fault, that I had failed them. I tried to gain their sympathy by justifying my actions. I explained that I had kept the 1200 guilders so that we could afford to put a new roof on the schoolhouse, and build a better playground. One of the students identified herself as the teacher and described how quiet and lonely the playground was now. I announced that we had to develop a plan for getting the children back. We decided we would paint a mural of our town. If the Pied Piper brought the children back, he would be able to find their homes on the mural.

At this point we came out of role and enjoyed an afternoon of painting. We decided not only to paint the homes and buildings of our town, but to add the missing children as well. This was the end of our first session and we decided that we would save the Story Drama for Friday afternoons because we were expecting a local guest artist who had worked with the class before, to attend our class then, and they didn't want her to miss any of it.

Session Two

During lunch hour the following Friday, Carole (our guest artist) and I put the mural of the town up around the classroom, so the children would see it and be reminded of our drama. Once they had settled in front of their "building," I started pacing. I grabbed a bell from the rhythm instrument box and began to ring it. They immediately came running from their places. I thanked them for coming and said that we were going to have to find a way to get in touch with the Pied Piper. We decided to take a count to find out exactly how many children were missing. We put a list together of each child and their age. One child was having a difficult time finding a way into the drama. I addressed him as "Timmy," and spoke to him as if he were the one child (in the story) who had not been able to keep up with the others. He accepted his special role with relief. It was decided that he was the only one who knew where the opening in the mountain had been. His knowledge was invaluable. After much discussion as to how to get in touch with the Pied Piper, we decided to write letters to tell him how sad our town had become.

This led to a very intense discussion about whether or not we should offer him the 1200 guilders. I explained about what a contract was and the obligations people should live up to when they enter a contract. Almost half of the townspeople felt that he had kept his part of the bargain and had a right to his money. However, another group suggested that it would be worthwhile to try to get the children back without giving up the money. I raised the problems that this solution might create, because what they suggested would not honor the contract. I reminded them that we had made an agreement in good faith and not upheld our side of the bargain. I wanted them to anticipate the results of their decisions and to consider their obligations as good community members. This discussion gave them time to reflect on the choices. It was a powerful learning experience for all of us to be involved in this problem-solving while still in the role of concerned parents and community members.

We finally decided to hold a vote and let the majority decide. The vote was in favor of sending the letters along with 1200 fake guilders in the hope that we would get the children back and still be able to put a new roof on the schoolhouse and build the playground. I warned them that there might be negative repercussions if we weren't altogether honest with the Pied Piper. It was decided that Timmy would lead us to the foot of the mountain where we would leave our letters. At this point we came out of role and Carole led a discussion about what they might write in their letters. The students also decided to draw pictures to show the Pied Piper how sad we were without our children. We spent the rest of the afternoon finishing the letters.

Session Three

Carole arrived Friday afternoon with a large, beautifully-colored shopping bag full of surprises for the day's drama. We began our session by reading the letters and giving them to Timmy to deliver. We watched as he carefully placed them on a rock at the far end of the school grounds. We all retreated into a hiding place and waited. Suddenly, one student announced that she had seen a child come and read the letters. Timmy and Carole went to see if anything else had been left at the spot. When they returned, Carole announced that she had found something near the rock. She held out a walnut shell and opened it up to find a tiny piece of rolled up paper. It contained a message telling us to go back to our town and there we would find something from our children. When we returned to our room, we looked inside the shopping bag and saw that it was labeled "For the parents of our town." Everyone sat on the rug and Carole showed us the things that were in the bag. There were shells, feathers, bread in the shape of a turtle, gingerbread cookies, scented soap, masks and many other fascinating items. Our drama continued for a number of sessions, until it came to a natural conclusion, a conclusion that will differ with each class. At the end of the drama activity, I summarized with the children the laws that had been broken, both by the Pied Piper and the people of the town. We discussed what happens when people disregard the law and don't consider the rights of others. We talked about some similar wrongdoings that might happen in our community and what effect that would have on us. We concluded with the idea that laws are necessary for our protection, and it is important that everyone obey the laws.

This is only a sample of the many possibilities that can be pursued with Story Drama. The joy of using this strategy is that instead of simply reading stories, we live them, and through them we can experience important principles that the children will not soon forget. The following is a compilation of stories which have a legal issue in them. They are all potential vehicles for a story drama exploration. As your experience with story drama grows, you will find that you can compile a list of your own stories from within your curriculum which will meet the needs of your children.

☞ For some stories, it is effective to read through to the end, and carry on a "story drama" from there. For others, it is more effective to stop at a certain point (or points) <u>within</u> the story.

Bibliography of Story Drama

Alexander, Lloyd, *The King's Fountain*, E.P. Dutton and Co., Inc., New York.

Summary: When a wise scholar, eloquent merchant and strong metalsmith fail, a poor man must take responsibility to address an injustice by the King. The King plans to build a great fountain in his palace courtyard. This will result in the loss of water to the village.

Issue: How can the poor man and the villagers persuade the King and those in power to provide good and just leadership and not abuse their power.

Stopping point: "He trudged home, hopeless and heavy-hearted, and told his neighbors and his family that he could find no one to stop the building of the fountain."

Bell, Anthea, *The Wise Queen* (a traditional European folktale), Picture Book Studio, Neugebauer Press, 1986.

Summary: In this story, a King asks his Minister to do a number of tasks which seem to be impossible. The Minister has a wise daughter who advises her father on how to carry out the King's wishes. When the King hears about this, he decides to marry the daughter and make her Queen. However, he instructs her never to interfere with his decisions in the Court of Law. One day, the Queen meets a young boy who lost his calf due to an error by the King in the Court of Law. She tells the boy to ask for another trial.

Issue: Property/ownership rights. Appealing a wrongful decision.

Stopping point: "My own cow bore that calf, but a man went to the King and claimed that his horse gave birth to it, and when the case came to trial the King believed him." "Ask for another trial," said the Queen . . .

Birch, David, *The King's Chessboard*, Dial Books for Young Readers, New York, 1988.

Summary: A King insists on giving a wise man a reward for a service he offered freely. To teach him a lesson, the wise man asks for what seems to be a simple reward, but which increases until the King is not able to honor his side of the bargain.

Issue: Contract Law – is a contract enforceable if one of the parties did not understand what he was agreeing to provide? Opportunity for a small claims court simulation/debate/Mock Trial on the legality of this contract.

Stopping point: "After a time the Queen said to him, 'You must ask the wise man to release you from your promise. It is the only thing to be done.'"

Calmenson, Stephanie, *The Principal's New Clothes*, Scholastic Inc., N.Y., 1989.

Summary: Mr. Bundy, the principal, is the sharpest dresser in town. The children don't want to miss a day at school because they want to see what he is wearing. Moe and Ivy offer to make him a one-of-a-kind suit which is special because "it is invisible to anyone who is no good at his job or just plain stupid." It finally takes a kindergarten student to admit what everyone else does not want to say: "The principal's in his underwear!"

Issue: Contract Law: The students of the school can decide to take Moe and Ivy to Small Claims Court to collect damages and the money their principal paid in good faith for the suit. He may have been vain and foolish, but Moe and Ivy were dishonest and did not honor the intent of the bargain (contract).

Stopping point: The end of the book

DePaola, Tomie, *The Mysterious Giant of Barletta*, Harcourt Brace Jovanovich, 1984.

Summary: The peaceful townspeople of Barletta must think of a plan to save their village from an invading army.

Issue: The people must creatively problem-solve together to come up with a non-violent plan to save their town and the peaceful way of life they value. This is an opportunity to explore the democratic process in decision making.

Stopping point: "No one even smiled, let alone waved at the Mysterious Giant. No children played."

Englander, Karen (translated from Karusa), *The Streets are Free* or sometimes called *Nowhere to Play*, Annick Press Ltd., 1985.

Summary: The children in the town of Caracus, Venezuela, have nowhere to play as the city grows and takes over the open fields and forests. The creeks and streams have become sewers! The children try to play in the streets but finally decide to go to the mayor and ask the city to make an empty lot into a playground. Their parents are too busy to help them. The children make a sign and petition City Hall. The bureaucrats make a show of agreeing to help as they fear bad publicity. But City Hall does not stand behind their promise! The children have to come up with another plan!

Issue: Environmental law/children's rights/responsibility of elected officials/power of the press.

Stopping point: "'What happened to our playground?' the children asked. The adults always gave the same answer: 'The politicians always promise but they never do anything.'"

Evans, Katherine, *The Boy Who Cried Wolf*, Albert Whitman and Co., Chicago, 1960. (there are many versions of this story available in public libraries and many of them would be appropriate)

Summary: A young boy jeopardizes the safety of the village by warning that a wolf is near when it's only a joke. The time comes when there really is a wolf and the villagers do not believe him and do not respond to his call.

Issue: Community responsibility/public safety/lying. The villagers must meet to decide what to do about this boy's pranks.

Stopping point: The end of the story.

Hoban, Russell, *The Dancing Tigers*, Jonathan Cape Publishers, London, 1979.

Summary: The Rajah and his servants set out to kill tigers. The tiger community decides they will not just sit back and accept this fate. They will try to come up with a plan to save their lives and their environment.

Issue: Environmental law/protection of endangered species.

Stopping point: "'Now listen to me', said the elder. 'My whole world-picture has suddenly changed. As long as the Rajah knew his place it seemed to me that I knew mine but now I can't think how I could have been such a fool!'"

Hughes, Monica, *A Handful of Seeds*, Lester Publishing Ltd., Toronto, Ontario, 1993.

Summary: When Concepcion's grandmother dies she has no one to look after her. She must move to the barrio in the city. Because her grandmother had taught her how to grow vegetables for food, Concepcion takes seeds with her to the barrio.

When she joins the other homeless children, they offer to teach her how to steal food from the merchants' stalls so she will survive. Concepcion decides to try to grow a garden in the barrio so she can teach the other children how to grow their own food so they won't have to steal.

Issue: Stealing, children's rights.

Stopping point: "'Stay with us. We will teach you how to pick garbage and sell it, and how to take food from the merchants' stalls without being seen!' 'That is stealing,' said Concepcion, surprised."

Karlins, Mark, *Salmon Moon*, Simon and Schuster Books for Young Readers, New York, 1993.

Summary: Sarah and her grandmother, Mrs. Mankowitz, have a good friend named Mr. Lutz. He works at the fish market. One day he sees the most beautiful salmon in the world laying on ice. It is still breathing! That night the three decide to sneak back to the market to rescue the salmon and return it to the ocean. As they dash madly through the streets in their pajamas with the salmon held carefully in their arms, they are chased by the owner of the market yelling "Stop the salmon thieves!" This wonderful story has a very magical ending.

Issue: Civil disobedience – breaking the law for a worthwhile cause. This story lends itself to a debate or Mock Trial simulation.

Stopping point: The end of the story.

Keeping, Charles, *Miss Emily and the Bird of Make-Believe*, Hutchinson of London, 1968.

Summary: Mister Jack Ratty catches city sparrows, paints them beautiful colors, and sells them as "birds of make-believe." Miss Emily discovers his deception and calls upon the children in the neighborhood to help her confront Mr. Ratty at the market-place.

Issue: Capturing wild birds and selling illegally, false advertising.

Stopping point: "Miss Emily picked up the bird cage and went to find the children. She wanted their help when she met Mister Jack Ratty. They marched in a crowd towards the market place, . . ."

Levine, Arthur A., *Pearl Moscowitz's Last Stand*, Tambourine Books – A division of
  William Morrow and Co., Ltd., New York, 1993.

Summary: Pearl and her sisters loved their street with the beautiful ginkgo
  trees. As Pearl got older and the neighborhood changed, the trees
  were cut down until finally there was only one left.
  Now the city was preparing for more progress. The last ginkgo
  tree was slated to be cut down. With the help of the many families in this varied multi-cultural neighborhood, it was time for
  "Pearl Moscowitz's last stand!"

Issue: Community involvement in neighborhood development, civic
  disobedience, lobbying elected officials, power of the media, protection of the environment

Stopping point: "With a bold but measured step she walked over to the tree and
  wrapped the chain around its trunk and hers. Then she had Ron-
  nie lock his lock. 'Now go get your mother,' Pearl told him."

Polacco, Patricia, *Applemando's Dreams*, Philomel Books, New York, 1991.

Summary: Applemando had a wonderful and very special talent. He dreamed
  lovely dreams in bright, beautiful colors. These dreams were special because the other children could see them floating in the air
  above Applemando's head! They loved his dreams!
  One rainy day all the brightly colored dreams got wet and stuck
  to the walls of the village buildings. The villagers thought the
  children were lying. They did not believe the story about
  Applemando's dreams. They said the children must be punished
  for painting all over their property without permission. It is not
  until Applemando's wonderful talent saves the lives of the children that the villagers learn to value the dreams.

Issue: Graffiti, vandalism, punishment, community service.

Stopping point: "'Someone has painted our houses and stores,' a voice called out.
  'Who did this?' an angry woman cried. 'I'll find who is responsible
  for this prank,' the Mayor said as he saw the crowd that had gathered. Then his eyes fell on the children. They were covered with
  Applemando's dreams. 'You,' the Mayor shouted, as he started toward them. 'What have you children done?'"

Pomerantz, Charlotte, *The Princess and the Admiral*, Addison-Wesley, Reading, MA,
  1974.

Summary: "This fable of an ancient time was suggested by an incident
  involving Vietnam and the Imperial Navy of Kublai Khan, in the
  thirteenth century."

The people of Tiny Kingdom were very poor farmers and fisher-
men. Because the country was so poor, no other power had ever
declared war on them. Their young but wise Princess, Mat Mat,
was excitedly planning a carnival and fireworks display to cele-
brate the past 100 years of peace. When she met with her three elderly advisors they had bad news. The celebration could not go
ahead as the fishing boats had reported a large fleet of ships of
war sailing towards the Tiny Kingdom. They would arrive in two
days.

Issue: Protection of property and lives, peace versus war

Stopping point: "'No forts, no soldiers, no weapons, no sinews of war (mused the
Princess). Clearly we shall have to rely on . . . other things.'"

Stevens, Kathleen, *Molly McCullough and Tom the Rogue*, Fitzhenry and Whiteside
Ltd., Toronto, 1982.

Summary: Tom Devlin made his living by outsmarting unsuspecting farmers.
He would find out who was the richest farmer in an area, scout
out the farmer's land, draw a treasure map of it and arrive at the
farm asking for a meal and a night's lodgings. During the evening
he would persuade the farmer to sell him a small piece of the
land, then purposely leave the treasure map out for the farmer to
find when he went to bed. Of course, the next morning the farmer
would say he changed his mind and demand the property back in
exchange for something to appease Tom.

Issue: Contract law, buying and selling land under false pretenses

Stopping point: "And the next morning the farmer would tell Tom he had changed
his mind: The land was not for sale and here was Tom's money
back. Tom always acted indignant. 'We struck a bargain. What
will your neighbors think when they learn you're a man who goes
back on his word?'"

Sussex, Rayner, *The Magic Apple*, Methuen Children's Books, London, 1979.

Summary: The selfish mayor of the town deceives the people by taking the
magic apple from Mrs. Potter's tree. Instead of wishing for a new
mill which everyone needed (as the old mill had burned down), he
wishes for the barrels in his cellar to be filled with gold.
The opportunity for the town to have one wish is therefore lost, as
it was a selfish wish.

Issue: What should the town decide to do about the actions of the Mayor
and how he has taken advantage of his elected position? How can

they work together to solve this problem in a democratic way? Can some good come from this situation?

Stopping point: "When the angry people realized that the Mayor had not wished for a new mill but for gold just for himself, they. . ."

Tayler, Barbara, *The Man Who Stole Dreams*, Women's Educational Press, Toronto, 1950.

Summary: The people of the village begin to realize that their sleep is being disturbed because someone is stealing their dreams. They discover it is an evil thin man who holds their dreams and will not give them back. He puts them on sale and expects the people to buy them if they really want them.

Issue: Does the thin man have the right to sell things he has not obtained in a fair manner? How do the people problem solve together to get their dreams back? Using the democratic court process, this would be an opportunity for a mock trial simulation.

Stopping point: "'No!' the thin man cried. '. . . I own all those dreams!'"

Vernon, Adele, *The Riddle*, Dodd, Mead and Co., New York, 1987.

Summary: Lost in the forest while on a hunting trip, the King is given food and water by a poor but content charcoal maker. He tells a riddle which greatly amuses the King. The King asks the charcoal maker not to tell the answer to the riddle to anyone else. He later becomes angry when he thinks the charcoal maker has broken his word.

Issue: Did the charcoal maker keep his part of the bargain? This presents an opportunity for a debate on the issue. Is it necessary to only follow the letter of the law, or is it also expected that one follows the intent of the law, also?

Stopping point: "'But I did,' grinned the charcoal maker, 'on each and every one of the hundred coins that the courtier gave to me!'"

Wildsmith, Brian, *The Tunnel*, Oxford University Press, Oxford, 1993.

Summary: An English mole named Marcus decides he would like to visit his cousin Pierre in France. They decide to tunnel under the English Channel. Some of the other animals think it's a good idea. Others say it will never work. The fish and other life in the water are afraid their environment will be damaged and their lives affected.

Issues: There are many different opportunities to explore issues such as meeting building requirements, dealing with bureaucrats, noise bylaws, rights of the community vs. rights of developers, fair compensation, "progress" vs. environmental protection.

Stopping point: This short, delightful bilingual storybook has opportunities to stop on almost every page, depending on which of the issues listed above you plan to explore.

Wildsmith, Brian, *The Owl and the Woodpecker*, Franklin Watts Inc., N.Y., 1971.

Summary: The animals of the forest try to resolve the problem between the owl and the woodpecker so that everyone can return to a peaceful co-existence. How do they solve the problem? The owl likes to sleep during the day, but the tapping of the woodpecker is annoying him and keeping him awake! Neither the owl or the woodpecker will agree to move to a different location.

Issue: The forest community must attempt to problem solve a solution to this dilemma. Perhaps there is a need to develop guidelines (laws) which will enable everyone in the forest to live together in harmony.

Stopping point: "He began to be so crotchety and rude that all the other animals decided something must be done. So they held a meeting."

Wildsmith, Brian, *Professor Noah's Spaceship*, Oxford University Press, 1980.

Summary: The forest and its environment are being destroyed by pollution. The animals must find a way to work together to save their world and put a halt to the pollution.

Issue: A community must work together to save their environment. An opportunity to study the impact of change and our environmental laws. Are they strong enough? Are they effective? How can individuals within a community work together to improve these laws?

Stopping point: "Lion sighed. 'My friends, we must do something. Our very lives are in peril. Does anyone have an idea what we should do?' "

Yolen, Jane, *The Seventh Mandarin*, The Seabury Press, New York, 1970.

Summary: A good King discovers that in order to rule it is necessary to know not only the laws of the land, but the people of his Kingdom, also.

Issue: Are all laws written down absolutely "right," and anything not written "untrue"?

Stopping point: "That very night, the King and his seven mandarins made their way to the. . . ." (village, to meet with the people to discuss how to better rule the Kingdom from then on.)

Zwerger, Lisbeth, (original by Oscar Wilde), *The Selfish Giant*, Picture Book Studio, Neugebauer Press, London, 1984.

Summary: The Selfish Giant returns after a seven year absence to find children playing in his garden. It is the only lovely and safe place for the children to play, yet he builds a tall wall around the garden and puts a "No Trespassing" sign on the gate.

Issue: The Giant is within his rights, as it is his garden, and the children must obey the "No Trespassing" law. However, can they come up with a plan which will change the Giant's mind so that he will open his garden to everyone?

Stopping point: "They used to wander round the high walls when their lessons were over, and talk about the beautiful garden inside. 'How happy we were there!' they said to each other. . . ."

✏ An additional example of a story book which can be used to explore legal issues by extending language arts activities:

Ahlberg, Janet and Allen, *The Jolly Postman or Other People's Letters*, William Heinemann Ltd., London, 1986.

Summary: The Jolly Postman brings the following mail:

1. To: The Three Bears

From: Goldilocks – an apology for eating bear's porridge, and breaking his chair

Issue: trespassing, theft

Activity: write "sentencing" reports from the Judge, "brainstorm" suitable community service for Goldilocks

2. To: Gingerbread Witch

From: Business advertising "Witch's Brew" products with money back guarantees if not completely satisfied

Issue: false advertising

Activity: small claims court simulation (witch vs. company) for false advertising

3. To: The Giant

From: Jack

Issue: trespassing and theft

Activity: Young Offender's Act, Mock Trial

4. To: Cinderella

From: Piper Press

Issue: advertising/copyright laws

Activity: students draw up a contract between Cinderella and Piper Press Publishers

5. To: Wolf

From: Little Red Riding Hood's solicitors

Issue: illegal occupation of another's property (Grandmother's cottage), trespassing

Activity: students write eviction notices, role play a Mock Trial

6. To: Goldilocks

From: Baby Bunting

Issue: postal laws, counterfeit money, children's rights

Activity: students write invitations and follow the process from point of mail to delivery and the laws protecting private mail, students study actual situations where counterfeit money was involved.

CHAPTER 6
Managing Peer Pressure Through Law-Related Literature

Margaret Ferguson

The concepts acquired through law-related education have many benefits, one of which is helping students to manage peer pressure. This chapter provides specific lessons using literature to develop these skills.

As concerned adults we acknowledge the importance of peer groups in the lives of young people, yet fear their negative influences. How do we develop in our students a strong sense of self and the ability to weather the constant pressures to conform? Law-related education can help children become more able to express their own feelings and opinions, more capable of evaluating information, able to recognize legitimate authority, positively manage conflict and more likely to internalize ethical values. This is because law-related education explores and develops in students an understanding of fundamental concepts such as authority, diversity, responsibility and justice. Law-related education explores decision-making processes and ways of resolving conflict, including methods other than "going to court." Law-related education also examines those values and attitudes that people should possess if they are to contribute positively to the functioning of a democratic society. And, most important, law-related educators have found appropriate ways of conveying these understandings, skills and attitudes, beginning with very young children.

Children's literature can be an invaluable ally in developing these competencies. Note how many successful authors refer to themselves as *outsiders*, as being different and often rejected by their peers when they were growing up. These authors don't shy away from reminding us, in their books, of how cruel children can be to each other. Furthermore, they do it much better than we can as teachers! The words and characters are carefully crafted, incidents that are rather ugly or painful are softened with humor, and the reader gets the message without having to hear a sermon! Furthermore, most novels used by a teacher in a classroom convey a sense of hope, that we CAN do better.

Realistic stories work well because the characters in realistic novels are often confronting the same sorts of conflicts with parents, teachers, siblings and friends as are the students in your classroom. Therefore, with little extra effort, one can extrapolate from the fictional situation to real life. Children can analyze the choices made by the characters in the novels, and readily apply what is learned to their own lives. Thus the book *mirrors* real life.

Perhaps even more important is the opportunity to expose children, through realistic novels, to situations and conflicts they have never encountered, and perhaps will never encounter. A well-written novel often results in children empathizing with characters they would never dream of associating with in real life. For a period of time, the reader can be literally placed in the shoes of someone very different. This exposure to people who are different, and yet the same, is invaluable in helping to develop a tolerance for difference, which, in turn, figures prominently in this theme of peer pressure. Thus the book is a *window* through which the children can look at a bigger world.

Concept Development

A number of important concepts arise within this general theme of peer pressure, including the concept of *friends*. In fact, friendship could serve as a unifying theme for planning all subsequent learning activities.

Other important concepts within this theme are *conflict, authority, diversity, responsibility* and *justice*. These concepts are not just legal concepts. Because they cross the conventional boundaries of subject areas, teachers can work on developing them in a number of different subject areas. Yes, these concepts may have a particular meaning in the legal world, and sometimes that will be the focus of the activities. However, the law also borrows values and ideas from religion, morality and science. The goal for students at this level is to extend their understanding of these concepts.

A modified "spider map" has been prepared for each of these six concepts. The information on these concept maps is certainly not meant to be all-inclusive, but it can be used as a tool for developing learning activities. In addition, these maps provide a quick visual reference for teachers. Note that the main ideas are located on the diagonal lines, while supporting ideas appear on the horizontal lines.

Concept: Authority

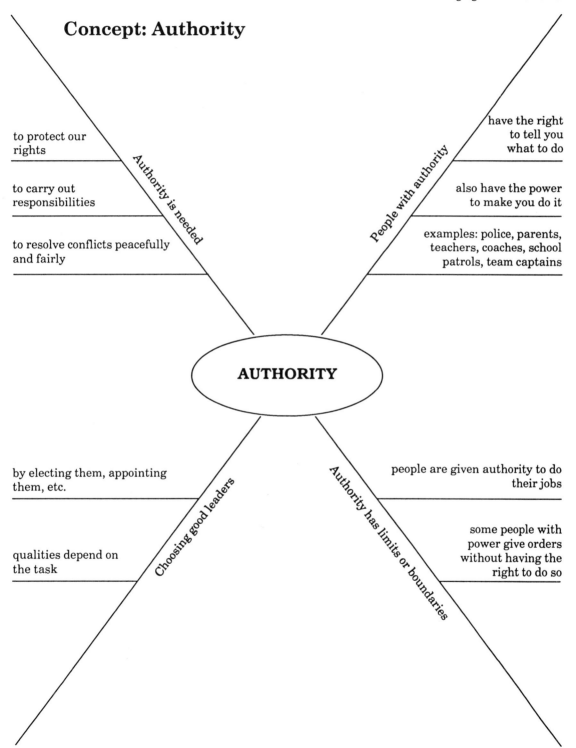

to protect our
rights

to carry out
responsibilities

to resolve conflicts peacefully
and fairly

Authority is needed

People with authority

have the right
to tell you
what to do

also have the power
to make you do it

examples: police, parents,
teachers, coaches, school
patrols, team captains

AUTHORITY

by electing them, appointing
them, etc.

qualities depend on
the task

Choosing good leaders

Authority has limits or boundaries

people are given authority to do
their jobs

some people with
power give orders
without having the
right to do so

Concept: Conflict

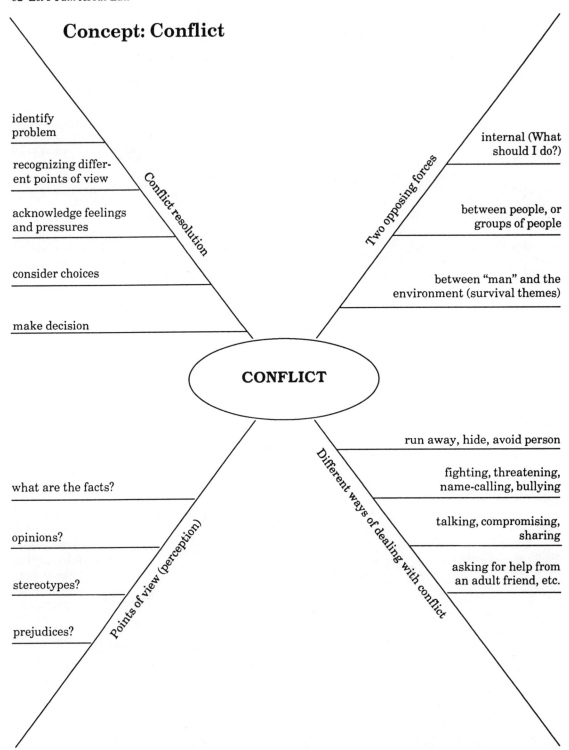

identify problem

recognizing different points of view

acknowledge feelings and pressures

consider choices

make decision

Conflict resolution

Two opposing forces

internal (What should I do?)

between people, or groups of people

between "man" and the environment (survival themes)

CONFLICT

run away, hide, avoid person

fighting, threatening, name-calling, bullying

talking, compromising, sharing

asking for help from an adult friend, etc.

Different ways of dealing with conflict

what are the facts?

opinions?

stereotypes?

prejudices?

Points of view (perception)

Concept: Diversity

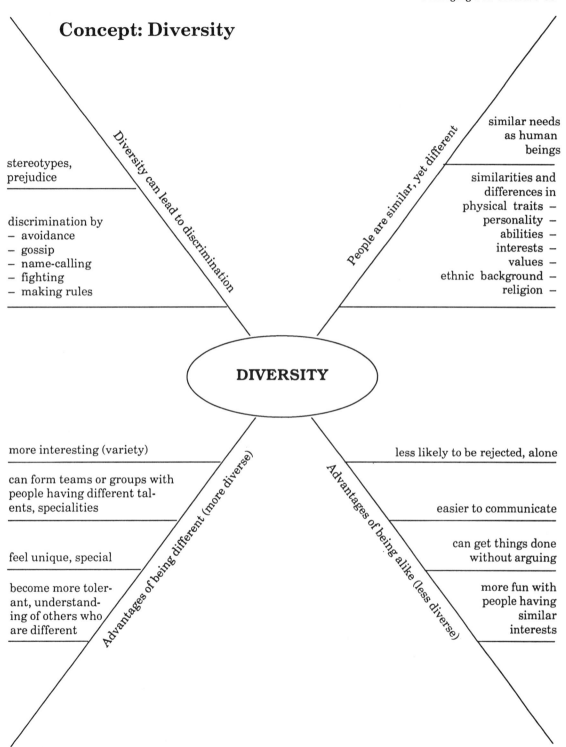

Diversity can lead to discrimination

stereotypes,
prejudice

discrimination by
– avoidance
– gossip
– name-calling
– fighting
– making rules

People are similar, yet different

similar needs
as human
beings

similarities and
differences in
physical traits –
personality –
abilities –
interests –
values –
ethnic background –
religion –

DIVERSITY

Advantages of being different (more diverse)

more interesting (variety)

can form teams or groups with
people having different talents, specialities

feel unique, special

become more tolerant, understanding of others who
are different

Advantages of being alike (less diverse)

less likely to be rejected, alone

easier to communicate

can get things done
without arguing

more fun with
people having
similar
interests

Concept: Friends

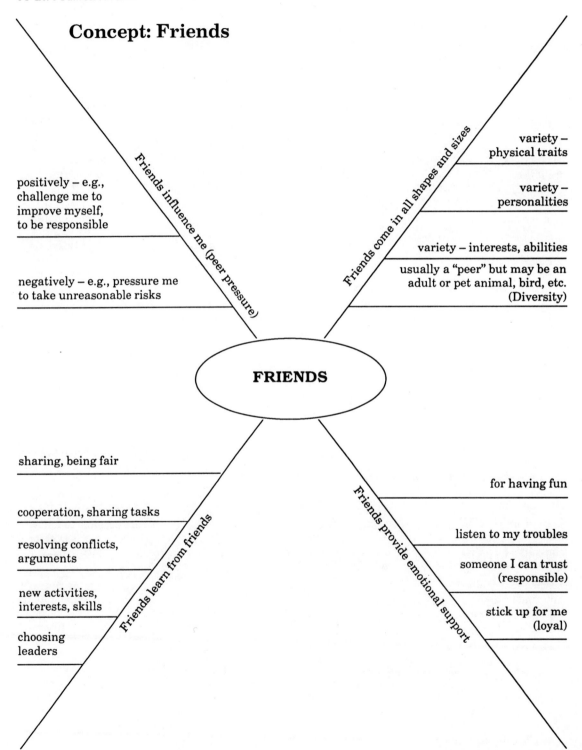

FRIENDS

Friends influence me (peer pressure)

positively – e.g.,
challenge me to
improve myself,
to be responsible

negatively – e.g., pressure me
to take unreasonable risks

Friends come in all shapes and sizes

variety –
physical traits

variety –
personalities

variety – interests, abilities

usually a "peer" but may be an
adult or pet animal, bird, etc.
(Diversity)

Friends learn from friends

sharing, being fair

cooperation, sharing tasks

resolving conflicts,
arguments

new activities,
interests, skills

choosing
leaders

Friends provide emotional support

for having fun

listen to my troubles

someone I can trust
(responsible)

stick up for me
(loyal)

Concept: Justice

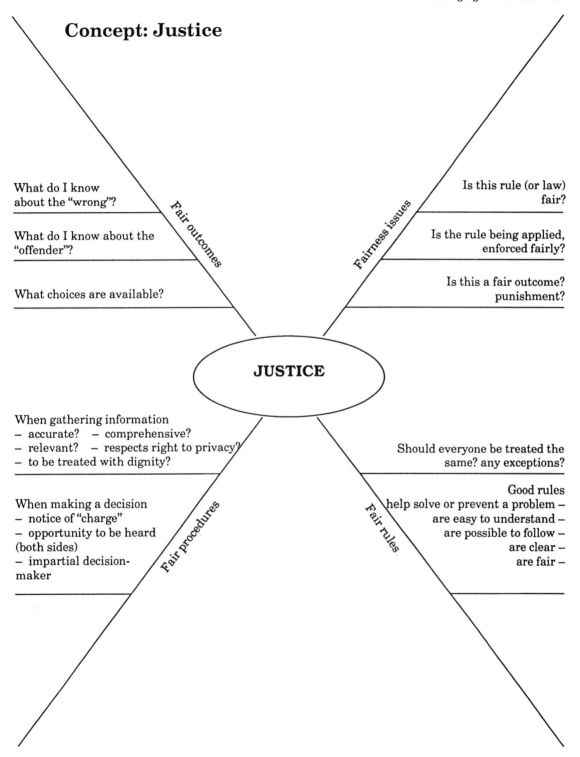

Fair outcomes

What do I know
about the "wrong"?

What do I know about the
"offender"?

What choices are available?

Fairness issues

Is this rule (or law)
fair?

Is the rule being applied,
enforced fairly?

Is this a fair outcome?
punishment?

JUSTICE

When gathering information
– accurate?   – comprehensive?
– relevant?   – respects right to privacy?
– to be treated with dignity?

When making a decision
– notice of "charge"
– opportunity to be heard
(both sides)
– impartial decision-
maker

Fair procedures

Fair rules

Should everyone be treated the
same? any exceptions?

Good rules
help solve or prevent a problem –
are easy to understand –
are possible to follow –
are clear –
are fair –

Concept: Responsibility

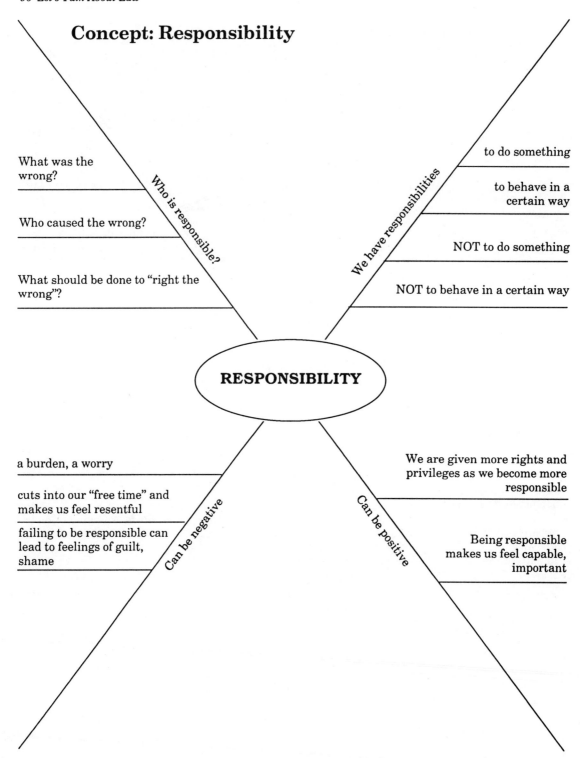

RESPONSIBILITY

Who is responsible?

What was the wrong?

Who caused the wrong?

What should be done to "right the wrong"?

We have responsibilities

to do something

to behave in a certain way

NOT to do something

NOT to behave in a certain way

Can be negative

a burden, a worry

cuts into our "free time" and makes us feel resentful

failing to be responsible can lead to feelings of guilt, shame

Can be positive

We are given more rights and privileges as we become more responsible

Being responsible makes us feel capable, important

Featured Literature

Seven books have been chosen to illustrate how discussions about law-related concepts might evolve. Consider these books as suggestions but keep in mind that there are many, many other books that are appropriate. Similarly, although realistic stories are featured in this chapter, other genres of children's literature also deal with the theme of friendship and concepts like authority, responsibility, justice and so on.

If you are unsure about what books to use, consult the librarian in your school, or the local public library. Librarians have access to lists of books that have won awards, and lists of books that children themselves recommend. Consider joining the local council of the International Reading Association as a good way to keep abreast of new teaching ideas, new books and new authors. Finally, contact the Canadian Children's Book Centre for its lists and publications.

The following books are featured in this chapter:

Books for younger readers (picture books)

- *The Quarreling Book*
- *The Hating Book*
- *The Pillow*
- *Crow Boy*

Books for older readers (chapter books)

- *On My Honor*
- *Harriet the Spy*
- *Cages*

An outlining device called a "Story Map" will give teachers a quick idea of what the book is about. Following each story map will be some questions and activities based on the friendship theme and the six law-related concepts.

Story Map

CONCEPTS: Authority, Conflict Resolution, Justice

BOOK: *The Quarreling Book* (1963); text by Charlotte Zolotow, illustrated by Arnold Lobel; Harper & Row Publishers.

MAIN CHARACTERS:

Mr. James	Sally James
Mrs. James	Eddie James
Jonathon James	Marjorie James
	"Dog"

PROBLEM:
Mr. James forgot to give his wife a kiss before going to work. This, plus the bad weather, made Mrs. James very cross.

Event: Mrs. James gets angry with Jonathon for wearing a dirty shirt.

Event: Jonathon ridicules Sally for being too slow.

Event: Sally makes unkind remarks to Marjorie about her raincoat.

Event: Sally calls her little brother Eddie a sissy.

Event: Eddie pushes the dog off his bed.

RESOLUTION:
Dog breaks this chain of scapegoating. The dog's good-natured re-action causes everyone to "make up" with the person he or she hurt.

The Quarreling Book by Charlotte Zolowtow

Concepts: Authority, Conflict Resolution, Justice

1. Was anyone acting "bossy" in this story – giving orders, telling someone else what to do? (Mrs. James?)
   Read a definition from the dictionary of the word AUTHORITY. For example, "the power or right to give orders and make others obey, or to take specific action." Do you suppose Mrs. James had a right to tell Jonathon to take off his dirty shirt? (Mrs. James had the authority to give this order because she was his mother and responsible for making sure he wore clean clothes to school.)

2. People with authority should still act fairly. Who acted unfairly in this story? Why do you think the behavior was unfair?

3. Other authority figures . . . list the places where children might go, such as school, the supermarket, the fire station, church, music lessons, swimming lessons and so on. Then list the "person in charge" at these places, such as teacher and principal, store manager, fire chief, minister, music teacher, lifeguard, etc. Discuss what sort of orders these people might have to give, as part of their jobs.

4. Sometimes people boss you around without having any right to do so. Examples? Jonathon bossing his sister Sally, Sally bossing Eddie. These people may have the power to make you obey (e.g., they are bigger than you) but they don't have authority.

5. Bring older students into class to talk about their responsibilities and what authority they have been given in order to carry out these responsibilities – e.g., school patrols, hallway monitors, team captains.

6. What does this playground chant mean?
   "Sticks'n'stones may break my bones but words can never harm me."
   Is it true that words don't hurt? How did words hurt Jonathon, Sally, Marjorie and Eddie?

7. What's a scapegoat? (Blaming or picking on someone for no good reason.) Were there any scapegoats in this story?

8. If you were lying on that bed, instead of the dog, which one of the following solutions would you try in order to stop the quarrelling?

☞ Count to ten, then walk away and cool off.

☞ Laugh, make a joke ("I love falling off beds . . .").

☞ Ask Eddie, "What's wrong?"

☞ Tell Eddie, "I feel angry when you push me off the bed for no reason . . ."

☞ Other possibilities?

9. It is difficult to tell someone how you are feeling if you don't know a lot of "feeling" words. Make a list of feeling words, like angry, happy, sad, cross, mad, sorry, frustrated, etc. This list could be hung in a "Time Out Corner" where students could go when they were frustrated and ready to explode.

10. The power of words . . . compile and distribute a list of names (include others that are in current use!). Have students sort into two categories: names they would like to be called and names they dislike.
    honey sweetheart handsome ugly fatso skinny dumbo smart mature mean nerd awesome cross-eyed spastic cheap snob foreigner

11. Read *The Berenstain Bears Get In A Fight* for another account of conflict resolution between family members.

12. Write about a fight you had that got out of hand. How did it end?

13. Extend this theme of "predicting consequences" in science activities.

Story Map

CONCEPTS: Conflict Resolution, Justice

BOOK: *The Hating Book* (1969); text by Charlotte Zolotow, illustrated by Ben Shecter; Harper & Row Publishers.

MAIN CHARACTERS:

        "I" (young girl)

        "she" (her best friend)

PROBLEM:

        "I hate hate hate my friend," says the little girl. And she'd rather die than find out why!

Event: Friend won't sit beside her on the school bus.

Event: Friend refuses her offer of a pencil in class.

Event: Friend didn't ask for help in washing the blackboard.

Event: Friend didn't choose her to be on the same basketball team.

Event: Friend didn't wait to walk home from school with her.

RESOLUTION:

        Turns out to be a problem in communication. Once this is resolved, they become friends once more.

The Hating Book by Charlotte Zolotow

Concepts: Conflict Resolution, Justice

1. Hate is a powerful emotion. "I hate you" is an insult. But, do you always mean it when you say this? Let's read this story to find out. (Class can chant, in unison, the verse "I hate, hate, hate my friend.")

2. Discuss the real meaning of "I hate my friend . . ."

☞ I was afraid of losing my best friend.

☞ I was confused because she seemed mad at me for no reason.

☞ I felt alone, ugly, dumb, worthless.

3. How did "the friend" behave to show she was angry or hurt?

4. The way you act or behave is one way of showing others how you are feeling. Have students, in pairs, choose an emotion to act out. Partner has to guess the emotion.

5. Make masks in art. Notice the cover illustration where children are wearing masks to try to cover up their emotions. In social studies, examine the role of masks in the Haida and other North American native cultures.

6. This book shows us some good ways of handling conflicts or "fights" with our friends. What are they?

➼ talking to an adult about the problem (mother)

➼ no screaming or name-calling to make matters worse

➼ walking away when necessary (turning the other cheek)

➼ confronting the friend, not giving up, taking responsibility for solving the problem

➼ talking it out.

7. Make a chart of **Ways to solve conflicts peacefully**. This could be placed in the "Time Out Corner" beside the feelings chart. It would serve as a reminder when real conflicts occur.

8. What is a fact? Give some examples. Compare these "facts" with the following definition:
   FACT: Something that is true or real. Something that you know for sure; something that has really happened; what something is or does. *Facts can usually be proven.*

9. How do we discover facts? We use our five senses: sight, hearing, taste, smell and touch. Have students list some facts about apples (e.g., apples are red, crunchy, hard, the size of a small ball, etc.). Discuss how students know this, what senses were used.
   Now, in partners, try to list some facts about your partner. These facts might include a physical description, as well as descriptions about interests, family background, pets and so on.

10. Extend this study of facts to other subject areas. In social studies, students can list facts about their neighborhood, province and so on. Similarly, the discovery of facts is a very important part of science.

11. Sometimes people say things that are what they think or feel. We call these OPINIONS. It is your opinion when you say "Apples are better in pies than eaten raw." Here are some other opinions you might have about apples: "McIntosh apples are the best." " Apples are too filling." "I hate green apples." "Apples are great for lunches."
    Have students give their opinion about . . . a school subject, a sport, a book they have read, this book (*The Hating Book*), a TV program, etc. Then have them give you a fact about each topic.

12. Sometimes problems develop because we treat opinions (what we think) as if they are facts (what is true). Are these statements (from *The Hating Book*) facts or opinions?

➼ You look like a freak.

- ✏ You're ugly.

- ✏ You're dumb.

- ✏ Being with you was never fun.

13. When real conflicts develop, have students relate, or write down, THE FACTS. See if they can refrain from giving opinions. (In law, judges are very reluctant to hear opinions. Opinions are not necessarily true and therefore it can be dangerous to base decisions on them.)

14. Watch commercials on television. Give examples of facts and opinions. Make your own commercial and include both facts and opinions.

15. In this book the problem was caused by a simple misunderstanding. "Sue said Jane said you said I looked like a freak." The truth? "I said you looked neat."
    There are many games (called telephone or gossip) which illustrate how words can be twisted or changed as they are passed along. Perhaps the students have their own examples.
    When this happens, how does one find out what was actually said? (Go to the person who made the statement). What is wrong about relying on gossip? (People can make mistakes in hearing; people can make mistakes in remembering what was said; people can make mistakes when it comes time to tell the story)
    In law, this type of gossip is called "hearsay" and such statements are not allowed in court.

16. This type of discussion could then lead into one about the need for writing down important rules (and laws). Are the important school rules in writing and in a place where students can consult them?

Story Map

CONCEPTS: Diversity, Responsibility

BOOK: *The Pillow* (1979); text by Rosemary Allison, illustrated by Charles Hilder; James Lorimer & Company, Publishers.

MAIN CHARACTERS:

Angelina	Ram
Grandma Rosa	Ram's grandmother

PROBLEM:

Angelina moves to Canada from Italy with her parents. She is lonely, afraid and misses her Grandma Rosa.

Event: Angelina's special pillow is snatched from her at school.

Event: Angelina meets Ram and his grandmother.

Event: Ram helps Angelina at school.

Event: Ram teaches Angelina some English words, including PILLOW.

Event: Angelina discovers a group of kids playing catch with her pillow.

RESOLUTION:

With Ram's help, Angelina recovers her pillow and begins to make some friends.

The Pillow by Rosemary Allison

Concepts: Diversity, Responsibility

1. In what ways was Angelina different from the other children at school? (She spoke Italian, didn't understand English, was a newcomer to Canada and didn't understand school routines.)

2. In what ways was Angelina similar to the other children at school? (She needed friends; felt good when people smiled at her; felt afraid when things were new and foreign to her; loved her grandmother; lived with her parents; liked to play.)

3. Why did Angelina bring the pillow to school? Have you ever brought something special to school? Why was it *different* when Angelina did this? (This is usually done by younger children. Nobody had experienced a pillow as being an object of affection.)

4. My favorite things: Listen to the song from the musical "The Sound of Music." Have students conduct their own survey of favorite things. Point out similarities and differences that exist in the class. Explain the meaning of DIVERSITY – the existence of differences, variety.

5. Ram assumed some responsibility for making Angelina feel welcome at school. Why do you think he did this? (Maybe because he had more information about her because he lived next door and his grandmother would tell him how she felt. Maybe because he was from India and knew what it felt like to come to a new country.)
    Who else had some responsibility to make Angelina feel welcome at school? (Her teacher, her parents and other kids.) Are adults as much help in these situations as other kids?

6. Sometimes children who change schools in the middle of the year feel just as unwelcome as Angelina. Have students discuss their ideas for welcoming new people. This book could be the starting point for listing some ways to act in this situation.

7. Angelina was finally able to communicate her anger when she kicked the boy. How do people communicate when they don't speak the same language? Try games like pictionary and charades.

8. Suppose you have just moved to Italy (or some other country being studied in Social Studies). Find out what your school will be like, what your house will be like, what food you will eat, how you will dress, etc. Use a data retrieval chart to organize the facts you discover in your research.

9. Read another book about a special pet or teddy bear, or velveteen rabbit! *The Sandwich* by Ian Wallace and Angela Wood describes an Italian boy who is teased for eating "stinky meat."

10. In this story, Angelina may not have known enough English to "tattle" on her classmates. Many children would, however. What is the difference between "tattling" and "responsible reporting"? One explanation is offered in *The Berenstain Bears Learn About Strangers.*
    Make a list of incidents to discuss. For example:

☞ not taking turns on the slide.

☞ throwing snowballs.

☞ pushing in the line-up at recess.

☞ taking someone's lunch.

☞ cheating on an exam.

   Help students learn to make good judgments about reporting incidents by having them consider:

☞ the possible consequences – to that person, to other people

☞ whether or not someone can be seriously hurt, or property can be damaged beyond repair

☞ whether or not the behavior is done "on purpose" or is an accident.

11. When problems result, and tattling occurs, examine the "rule." Is it fair? Is it a good rule, meaning it is easy to understand, possible to follow, clear and workable (solves the problem)?

Story Map

CONCEPTS: Diversity, Responsibility, Justice

BOOK: *Crow Boy* (1955); text by Mitsu and Taro Yashima; Picture Puffins, Penguin Books Canada

MAIN CHARACTERS:
              Chibi or Crow Boy

Children at village school
Mr. Isobe

PROBLEM:

A strange, shy boy is isolated by his differences.

Event: This boy is nicknamed Chibi or "tiny boy."

Event: Chibi is ignored by his teachers and taunted by his classmates.

Event: Chibi learns to amuse himself for hours on end.

Event: Mr. Isobe, the sixth grade teacher, takes an interest in Chibi.

Event: Chibi's special knowledge and talents are discovered.

RESOLUTION:

Chibi's remarkable imitation of the voices of crows at a school talent show is the turning point. Chibi wins respect and a better name, Crow Boy!

Crow Boy by Taro Yashima

Concepts: Diversity, Responsibility, Justice

1. Facts and opinions about Chibi: Put an "F" next to each statement that is a FACT. Put an "O" next to each statement that is an "OPINION".
    (F) The nickname Chibi means "tiny boy."
    (F) Chibi attended a Japanese village school.
    (O) Chibi was a slowpoke and stupid.
    (O) Chibi could not make friends.
    (O) Chibi was cross-eyed because he couldn't understand anything.
    (F) The kids and teachers ignored Chibi at school until Grade 6.
    (O) Chibi will never be able to learn.
    Note that some opinions are better than others! People are more likely to believe you when you have some facts to justify your opinion. For example, it might be your opinion that Chibi is the best imitator of crows in the country. You could then prove how many different ways he could imitate a crow. It might be your opinion that Chibi could not learn because he was too afraid. If you could support this opinion with facts, most people would accept it as being true. Another opinion that could be supported by facts was that Chibi had remarkable powers of observation.

2. In this story the statement is made that the kids wronged Chibi. How did they wrong Chibi? (They ignored him, talked about him, called him names, etc.) Do classmates have some responsibility to try to make "outsiders" feel welcome?

3. Mr. Isobe was Chibi's first friend, as well as being his teacher. What did Mr. Isobe do to become friends with Chibi?
    Can the following opinion be supported by facts?

Mr. Isobe thought that Chibi had some unique talents and that others could learn from him.

4. A lot of people (students, teachers, parents) judged Chibi to be slow and stupid. They also knew he lived outside the village. Suppose, then, that another little boy who also lived outside the village came to school. Would you be tempted to think this boy slow and stupid, too? STEREOTYPING occurs when we draw conclusions based on one or two experiences. (All boys who live outside the village are slow and stupid.) We all stereotype. However, stereotypes can be unfair.
Here are some stereotypes people have. What is unfair about them?

✏ All girls with blond hair are dumb.

✏ Girls are not as good as boys at math.

✏ Boys have messy printing.

✏ Little children are crybabies.

✏ Kids who don't wear designer clothes are poor.
Are these statements always true? Could these stereotypes cause you to treat someone unfairly? Give examples of other stereotypes.

5. Chibi was renamed CROW BOY, a name he seemed pleased with. This name told people that he had a talent, that he was unique. Native American names are also symbolic. What name might you have in such a culture? Have students create new names for each other. These names must be positive and must tell something about the individual.

6. The law recognizes that people can become very attached to their names. Each person in the class has a legal name, which is usually the one given at birth. Some children who have been adopted may now have a different legal surname than that given at birth. At a certain age, however, a child must consent to any change in his or her name. The law also states how names can be legally changed. Sometimes parents make a mistake in spelling the child's name at birth and they have to legally change it!
Have students report on the history of their name.

7. Read aloud excerpts from Jean Little's autobiographical book, *Little by Little*. In Grade 2, Jean was with a group of children who all had special needs and who all felt like Chibi – useless. A very sensitive teacher had the students weave a basket, something that they thought was impossible for them to do. This achievement made them feel very good about themselves. Later, Jean describes her battles as a child in a hostile Grade 4 classroom. Although Jean had very supportive teachers and parents, she gradually discovered that she had to fight and win her own battles.

Story Map

CONCEPTS: Conflict Resolution, Responsibility, Justice

BOOK: *On My Honor* (1968); text by Marion Dane Bauer; Clarion Books

MAIN CHARACTERS:

       Joel   Tony

       Joel's parents   Tony's parents

       Joel's brother, Bobby

PROBLEM:

       Joel's best friend Tony is pressuring him to do something crazy and dangerous – climb the rock bluffs in a nearby state park. Joel doesn't like being called a "chicken."

Event: Joel's dad reluctantly gives him permission to go to the park.

Event: Tony changes his mind, wants to swim in the river.

Event: Joel gives in, challenges Tony to swim to a sandbar.

Event: Tony drowns.

Event: Joel lies to his parents and the Zabrinskys – but admits the truth to the police.

RESOLUTION:

       Joel talks to his father about his feelings of guilt. His father reminds him that they all made choices, and will have to live with these choices.

On My Honor by Marion Dane Bauer

Concepts: Conflict resolution, Responsibility, Justice

Note: This story conveys a powerful message about the consequences of negative peer pressure (being forced to take unreasonable risks). Peer pressure is like conflict. It's something we can't escape, and can be positive, but we need to learn to recognize and then manage it. Since this story can be scary, teachers may want to read it aloud.

1. Read *The Berenstain Bears and the Double Dare*. This short book is a good introduction to the pressure exerted by peers in the form of dares (to take risks).

✍ What does it mean to dare someone? (to issue a challenge)

✍ Give some examples of dares.

✍ Why do we accept dares? (We want to prove we have courage. It makes us feel proud if we succeed, others might respect us more, and we test ourselves and find out what we are capable of doing.)

☞ What are some bad things about dares? (We are under pressure and don't have much time to think. Others are usually watching, sometimes there is nothing to gain by taking the dare and it can be dangerous – people can get hurt.)

2. Tony and Joel were best friends. Sometimes the dares made by best friends are very hard to resist. Why?

☞ What dares did Tony make? (to climb the rock bluffs, to swim in the river)

☞ What dares did Joel make? (to swim to the sandbar)

3. What is the meaning of **peer pressure**? (Influence or persuasion coming from someone who is equal in rank, age or ability. There can be positive or negative consequences to succumbing to peer pressure.)
   Were Joel and Tony peers? (yes) Do your peers have to be your friends? (no)
   Give some examples of how your friends or peers might try to pressure or influence you.
   (Pressure can be with words, actions or gestures – for example, name-calling such as "chicken, crybaby"; threats such as "if you don't do this you can't join our club"; harassment; rewards.)
   In partners, role play a situation where you are trying to influence your partner to do something he or she doesn't want to do.

4. Joel knew that there were risks involved and he felt these risks were NOT reasonable. He knew some FACTS about the rock bluffs and the river that helped him come to the conclusion that the risks involved danger.
   UNREASONABLE RISK: a situation you know is dangerous. A situation where you gain nothing positive if you succeed but, if you fail, you could lose something of great value.
   List some facts Joel knew about climbing the rock bluffs.
   List some facts Joel knew about swimming in the river.

5. Discuss: when dares are made, we have choices. We can accept the dare or we can refuse the dare. We are, however, responsible for the choices we make.
   Joel's father says it better: "We all made choices today, Joel. You, me, Tony. Tony's the only one who doesn't have to live with his choice" (p. 88).
   (Accepting responsibility is not easy, even for adults. How often do we hear comments like, "It's not my fault" or "She's to blame"!)

6. Whenever we fail to act responsibly, or when we feel responsible for something awful happening, we have tremendous feelings of guilt and shame. Describe how the feelings of guilt and shame affected Joel's behavior after the accident. Why did Joel feel responsible?
   Who else may have felt responsible for what happened? (Joel's father, Tony's parents, the teenagers.) Why?
   Was Tony also responsible? (Yes. This exercise of apportioning responsibility is

something civil courts do in every case of negligence. Often more than one person is responsible for the harm done. People who have contributed to their own injuries are awarded less money or compensation.)

7. Brainstorm ways of saying "NO" to an unreasonable risk. (Walk away, pose alternatives, go to an adult for guidance, etc.)
   How did Joel try to say "NO"? Role play other ways Joel might have handled the two dares.

8. Hold a public inquiry. The purpose of a public inquiry is not to find fault, but rather to investigate the cause of the injury and make recommendations to prevent similar accidents in the future.
   Issue a "subpoena" (a formal order requiring Joel to attend the inquiry). The student who is acting as "Joel" will swear an oath to tell the truth before taking the witness stand. (Failure to tell the truth in court can result in charges of perjury and sometimes imprisonment.)
   Students prepare questions for "Joel." (e.g., What is your name? How old are you? How long had you known Tony? What happened on the day in question?)
   After the inquiry is concluded, have students make recommendations (e.g., better signs warning of dangers of swimming, somebody watching the rock bluffs to prevent kids from climbing, etc.)

9. Physical education. Bring in a guest speaker to talk about water safety. A scuba diver might be able to describe how currents in a river affect a swimmer. Bring in an athlete to talk about how she/he manages to control the risks in his or her sport.

10. Joel wonders why his father doesn't punish him. Why do we punish people? (It is fair to penalize people who do something wrong because it might stop others from doing the same thing, it might stop the person being punished from repeating the act and it serves to reward those who follow the rules). In this case, do you agree with Joel's father that Joel does not need any more punishment?

11. Have your students write an anonymous "Ann Landers" type of letter seeking advice about a problem they are having with peer pressure. Letters can be collected in a box, and periodically discussed by the class.

Story Map

CONCEPTS: Justice, Diversity, Responsibility, Authority, Conflict Resolution

BOOK: *Harriet the Spy* (1964); written and illustrated by Louise Fitzhugh; HarperCollins Publishers Ltd.

MAIN CHARACTERS:

    Harriet Welsch   Janie Gibbs

Sport	other classmates
Ole Golly	

PROBLEM:

Harriet single-mindedly pursues her ambition to become a writer. She spies on people and writes down her observations in a series of notebooks. One day her classmates discover what she has written about THEM!

Event: Ole Golly marries and leaves the Welsch household.

Event: Harriet loses her notebooks.

Event: Classmates and best friends isolate Harriet and seek revenge.

Event: Harriet's parents seek help (school, doctor)

Event: Ole Golly writes to Harriet with some important advice.

RESOLUTION:

Harriet, in her capacity as Grade 6 editor for the school newspaper, apologizes for her "lies." Sport and Janie become her friends once more.

Harriet the Spy by Louise Fitzhugh

Concepts: Justice, Diversity, Responsibility, Authority, Conflict Resolution

1. Harriet's best friends at school are Sport and Janie. In what ways are these three friends similar? (They are career-oriented, independent thinkers, bright, have no siblings, etc.). In what ways are they different? (They have different interests, socio-economic backgrounds, personalities, etc.).

2. Create a survey on friendships. What questions do you want to include on this survey? (Do you have a best friend? How long has that person been your best friend? etc.)

3. Harriet's ambition was to be a writer. Like many writers, Harriet's desire to know things about people conflicted with their desire for privacy. How did "Harriet the Spy" invade other people's privacy? Do you think she ever broke the law when she was on her spy route? (Yes, breaking and entering into a private home).

4. Invite a journalist to talk to the students about "ethics" in investigative reporting. Are there any rules to ensure fair ways to gather information?

5. Analyze some of the remarks Harriet made about her friends and classmates. Why do you think these children were so hurt by her remarks? Did Harriet include facts as well as opinions in her notebook? Did she have facts to support her strong opinions or did she sometimes rely on gossip? (e.g., her mother's comments about people.)

6. After discussing fair ways of gathering information, students are given the assignment of "Spy for the Week." They map out a route, or a series of observation points (e.g., on the bus, at the local grocery store, on the playground) and record their observations in a green or yellow notebook just like Harriet used. These observations do not have to be about people.

7. Another variation is to have the student spies look for conflicts. They must report only what they see and hear. Devise a chart, recording the following items for each conflict:

☞ who is involved?

☞ where did the conflict occur?

☞ what is being done or said?

☞ how does the conflict end?

8. Do you think all Harriet's problems with her classmates stemmed from the discovery of the notebook? In what ways was Harriet an "outsider" or different from her classmates? Why might Harriet want to remain "different" from the others?

9. Harriet's friends and classmates wanted to "get even" with Harriet because her comments had hurt them. What were some of the things they did to her? Harriet, in turn, got hurt and wanted to seek her own revenge. Examine the list of things Harriet planned when she intentionally became "mean" (Chapter 13).
Discuss why revenge is an unsatisfactory way to resolve conflicts. (It results in one-upmanship; the stakes get higher; more people can get hurt; and the conflict generally escalates beyond all reason.)
The law offers a nonviolent alternative to revenge by providing courts and a process for resolving conflicts. Negotiation, mediation and arbitration are also alternatives.

10. The class elected an officer each year. Would you say this officer was a "person in authority"? (yes). What were the duties or responsibilities of the class officer?

11. The class officer was elected by the students. Why did Harriet never win the election? What other ways can leaders (or officers) be chosen? (By drawing names out of a hat; by teacher appointing the officer; by setting up a contest and choosing the winner; by requiring the group to come to an agreement or consensus but not by voting, etc.).

12. What improvements would you make to this election procedure? (Create more than one position such as officer and editor. Have elections for each position. Have a secret ballot so there is no chance of peer pressure and possible retaliation. Have candidates make a short speech in which they talk about their qualifications for the position.)

13. Being pressured by her peers was not a big problem for Harriet. However, being pressured by all of them as a group was scary. Discuss the power of groups and organizations.

14. Create an imaginary club and design some club rules, keeping these guidelines for "good rules" in mind:
    GOOD RULES:

✏ help solve or prevent a problem

✏ are clear

✏ are easy to understand

✏ are possible to follow

✏ are fair

Story Map

CONCEPTS: Responsibility, Justice, Authority

BOOK: *Cages* (1991); text by Peg Kehret; Pocket Books

MAIN CHARACTERS:

Kit Hathaway	Mrs. Fenton
Marcia	Kit's mother
Tracy	Kit's stepfather, Wayne

PROBLEM:

Kit steals a bracelet (worth $149) after finding out that Marcia was chosen for the lead role in a school play, rather than her.

Event: The store security officer calls the police and Kit's mother.

Event: Kit tells Tracy she can't go to Tracy's birthday party.

Event: Kit is sentenced by the Juvenile Court Diversion Committee.

Event: Kit's plan to find a home for "Lady" fails.

Event: Kit decides to reveal her "secret" to Tracy and all her classmates.

RESOLUTION:

Kit's responsible behavior earns her a second chance. She wins the coveted Grade 9 scholarship, and keeps her best friend Tracy.

Cages by Peg Kehret

Concepts: Responsibility, Justice, Authority

1. Kit's best friend is Tracy. In what ways is Tracy similar to Kit? In what ways is she different?

2. The opening chapter reveals Kit's dilemma. A DILEMMA is a situation where a person has to make a choice, and each choice has unpleasant consequences. What was Kit's dilemma? (to refute Arthur, reveal her secret and lose Tracy as a friend *or* to ignore Arthur's challenge, lose marks and maybe her chances at getting the Grade Nine Scholarship)

3. Why did Kit decide to steal the bracelet? Was it peer pressure, or were there other reasons?

4. In every conflict between people there are at least two points of view. In this book, Kit has conflicts with Marcia, her mother, Wayne and even Tracy. We know Kit's point of view, but what might the other person be thinking or feeling? Identify a conflict between Kit and some other person, then describe that *other* person's point of view. For example:

Wayne: Kit makes me so angry I can't help calling her an Animal. . . .

Marcia: I try to be friends with Kit but it isn't easy. . . .

Mother: Kit's behavior is getting worse every day. . . .

5. Once Kit stole the bracelet, she was no longer free to do as she pleased. Other people had the right to tell her what to do. Name these people with authority (store security, police officer, juvenile court diversion committee, manager of the humane society).

6. There are limits to a person's authority. Do you think the following statements are TRUE or FALSE?
    (F) A store security officer can charge people with shoplifting. (Only police officers can lay charges.)
    (T) A police officer can decide whether to charge people with shoplifting or let them go with a warning. (Often people in authority have a certain amount of discretion.)
    (F) In Canada, a police officer can decide to send a young offender to an alternative measures program. (This decision rests with the Crown Prosecutor.)
    (F) The Juvenile Court Diversion Committee could send Kit to jail if appropriate. (Any person committing a crime where jail is a possibility would have to go to court. These alternative programs are for less serious offences and the sentencing options are restricted.)
    (T) The manager of the humane society can decide what work Kit will do for her 20 hours of community service.

7. This story takes place in the United States. Discuss similarities and differences in the criminal laws of Canada and the United States.

Similarities and Differences:

✏ Shoplifting is a criminal offence (called theft in Canada)

✏ The value of the object stolen is an important factor. (In Canada, theft over $2000 is a more serious offence than theft under $2000. In this book, theft over $250 was a more serious offence than theft under $250.)

✏ There are two major classifications of criminal offences. (In the United States, serious offences are called felonies. In Canada they are called indictable offences. In the States, less serious crimes are called misdemeanors. In Canada they are called summary conviction offences.)

✏ Police officers are required by law to remind young people who are charged with a crime of their legal rights. (In the United States, the Miranda case established the need to read accused persons their rights. This is referred to in the book on page 29. In Canada the warning is slightly different, but is also a requirement of law.)

✏ Young people who commit crimes can sometimes avoid going to court. (In this book, the Juvenile Court Diversion Committee handled Kit's case. In Canada, the Young Offenders Act authorizes alternative measures programs. Each local area may set up such a program.)

8. Kit made a decision – to steal a bracelet – and there were consequences. Make a list of the consequences (e.g., she loses her self-respect and has feelings of guilt. She needed to be secretive and was questioned by store security and police. She had to attend a hearing, do 20 hours of community service, and pay the store $300.)

9. This is a story about responsibility. Kit accepted responsibility for her decision. She was also given certain responsibilities to fulfill as part of her punishment, and these responsibilities had a positive effect on Kit. In what ways did Kit change for the better?

10. Invite a police officer, or a speaker from youth service agency to talk about the law relating to young offenders and the alternative measures programs that are in place in your community.

11. Suppose this incident happened in your town. Kit is going to Youth Court. You are a Youth Court worker. It is your responsibility to fill out this report and then make a short presentation to the judge. The purpose of this report and presentation is to help the judge learn more about the offender. It is only fair that this information be considered before the offender is punished. In real life, the youth worker must interview family members, teachers, friends, and so on. Here you can use information obtained from the book.

REPORT ABOUT KIT HATHAWAY

Age

Charge

Family Background

Activities/Interests

School Record

Youth's Plans

Youth's Behavior/Attitude

Conclusion

Richard Peck, a very successful author for young adults, notes that *"few [teenagers] have any mechanism for challenging the rules of their peers."* Peck deliberately crafts his novels so that *"the steps the protagonist takes toward maturity are away from the peer group."* In fact, Peck claims that the power of the peer group is one factor that keeps him writing. He believes that *"good books give them something better to believe in."*[1]

"Little by little, I was sorting out when and whether belonging really mattered."[2] These are the words of Jean Little, in her powerful autobiography *Little By Little: A Writer's Education*. Jean's poor eyesight made her an easy target for bullies and cruel remarks. Ironically, Jean discovers that words are the source of her power. Jean recounts some hilarious incidents in this book: telling a big whopper to her Grade 5 teacher, knitting a "useless chain" in a home economics classroom, playing an intramural basketball game at university. Your students deserve to hear the lessons contained in Jean Little's story.

---

[1]*Literature for Today's Young Adults* by Kenneth L. Donelson and Alleen Pace Nilsen, third edition, Scott, Foresman and Company, 1989, at page 226.

[2]*Little by Little: A Writer's Education* by Jean Little, Penguin Books Canada Limited, 1987, at page 153.

CHAPTER 7
Making Law in the
Primary Classroom

Lois Klassen

The learning experiences described in this chapter are designed to introduce the very basic concepts of law and law-making to young children in the practical context of the classroom,

Very young children can begin to see themselves as participants in the regulation of their own lives as teachers help them appreciate the necessity for rules in social situations, and learn about the rules that protect them in their school and community. Another part of this chapter focuses on the concepts of fairness and justice with specific activities emphasizing tolerance, respect and acceptance of others.

After participating in the learning experiences of this unit students will:

- appreciate the need for rules;

- know the rules of the school and some of the pedestrian and bicycle traffic rules of the neighborhood;

- understand that some rules are better than others and know what the qualities of a good rule are, namely it:

  - is clear and understandable
  - can be followed
  - is enforceable
  - doesn't contradict other rules
  - has a penalty for non-compliance
  - is non-discriminatory (fair);

- appreciate that rules reflect needs and values of the group;

- understand that rules can be made, deleted and amended as needs and values change;

be able to cooperate with others to draw up a few simple rules for the classroom;

be able to review the above rules, after some time has passed, and work together as a group to assess their worth and effectiveness, making amendments, deletions or additions.

Learning Approach

This chapter is organized as a teaching unit, made up of nine topics using a variety of teaching strategies in a number of subject areas. There is some direct teaching of facts, some guided exploration and discoveries, some cooperative group work, some large group discussion, storydrama, visiting resource people, etc. Curriculum areas include language arts (through relevant books and stories, and also through discussion and writing), fine arts (through visual art projects and drama), physical education (through invented games), mathematics (through the classroom traffic activity in Topic 3) and science (through the topic of our environment).

Rationale

From birth a person's life is regulated by external agencies. The policies of the hospitals in which we are born determine when we eat, sleep and how much contact we have with our mothers. The less formal, but nonetheless powerful, structure of the family also regulates our life-rhythms – eating, sleeping and waking – and our social contacts. Our first tentative explorations of the world around us reveal imposed barriers to our freedom; the word 'No!' intrudes at every turn. We learn the boundaries which circumscribe our lives. We learn to ask permission. The circle of authority grows as we mature and grow; it expands to include not only our parents but also school and community authorities, and so on.

By the time children have spent a few years in school they have lived under the jurisdiction of others to the extent that they may think of rules and regulations (if they consciously think about them at all) as something inherent in life – something as pervasive as grass or sky, and just as impersonal. Without some instruction in the basic principles of law, few children will have gained an understanding of the most fundamental concepts of law and law-making; few will have grasped, for example, that laws/rules are made by people like themselves to ensure the greatest personal freedom for the greatest number and/or to protect the defenseless.

There is no doubt that children (and adults as well) often find the restrictions imposed on them by rules and regulations inconvenient and at cross-purposes with their own desires and immediate goals. They may as a consequence feel that authority (embodied in the great anonymous rule-makers) is somewhat arbitrary and antagonistic. That is not to say that children lack a relationship with the underlying principles of law, for children, like adults, frequently find themselves in situations of conflict – situations which 'the law' attempts to address. And finding themselves in these situations children send up their cries for justice: 'It's not fair!', 'He hit me first!', 'It's not your turn!' The fact that they are appealing for justice implies that they already possess a fierce, innate sense of what justice is. But having an innate sense of justice does not guarantee a conscious understanding of the workings of an institutionalized justice system, whether that system is a set of school rules, the Criminal Code or the courts.

Children need to know not only that there are rules, but what those rules are, who made them and why they were made (and, of course, what the consequences of breaking the rules are). They need to know that laws/rules are based on society's (or any group of people's) values and needs, that laws made by people can also be changed by people as their values and needs change, and that laws must be fair and non-discriminatory.

Armed with a knowledge of the principles behind law-making, children can begin to participate in the regulation of their own lives. They can help to make up classroom rules, for example. They can learn, and appreciate the need for, safety rules, for another example. Knowledge and understanding are tools to help children make sense of their world. A large part of a child's world is made up of rules and regulations. We owe it to them to help make sense of this aspect of their lives. A knowledge of law and law-making will give children an appreciation of their rights as individuals and of their responsibilities toward others. It will empower them to live as active participants, as citizens, in their world.

Topic #1 Do We Need Rules?

Objectives	Children will learn that pre-established guidelines and rules for behavior are often necessary to prevent conflict in society (or among groups of people, e.g. the classroom).
Intended Outcome	Children will appreciate the need for rules in the classroom and the school.
Materials and Resources	'It's Not Fair!' videocassette, 19 min. British Columbia: People's Law School, 1983.
Activities	Show the video. Have a short discussion to determine if children have grasped the message of the need for rules in our society. Extend the discussion to include the school and classroom. Have children imagine possible sources of conflict in the classroom. How would a

rule prevent this conflict?

Children write a short paragraph stating why they think rules are necessary and important. (Younger children may draw a picture based on the video).

Alternative Activities Play the game 'Eraser.' The teacher hands a blackboard eraser to one child in each group then announces enthusiastically, 'Play the game!' When children are unable to proceed teacher introduces the notion of the need for rules. This activity can be extended; children invent their own game of 'Eraser' and play it.

Or: assign an art project (e.g., make hand puppets) in which the supplies and equipment must be shared. Have children anticipate problems and make up rules to prevent them ahead of time.

Topic #2 What Are Our Rules?

Objective Children will work together to compile a list of the school and classroom rules, and then compare their list to the official list.

Intended Outcome Children will become familiar with the school and classroom rules.

Materials A list of the school rules, chart paper and felt pens, tag board for a poster.

Activities Children divide into small groups of three or four and brainstorm all of the school rules (and classroom rules) which they know. Groups report back to the class – a class list is compiled. Teacher then provides the official school rules and the lists are compared. Discuss, as a class, the possible reasons behind each rule. What problem, need or value does the rule address?

Children then prepare a poster of the school rules for the classroom wall. (This activity can be extended to include decorating the borders of the poster with artwork – either repeating patterns, or illustrations.)

Evaluation Children write a sentence or two listing the school rules which they had not known about until this activity.

Topic #3: Traffic and Safety Rules

General Remarks
This topic is the largest in the unit and could be expanded to form a unit of study on its own.

Objectives
Children will become familiar with and understand the community traffic laws; understand that technological changes can create changes in the environment which may necessitate new rules; see that rules must have penalties for non-compliance in order to be effective; think about other safety rules; become aware of the justice system.

Intended Outcomes
Children will know what is expected of them on the sidewalks and streets of their neighborhood. They will know the meaning of signs and traffic controls in their neighborhood. They will appreciate that rules are based on the needs of society and that rules protect us and help to preserve order.

Materials and Resources
Book: *Tin Lizzie* by Peter Spier, New York: Doubleday, 1975
Films: 'Every Dog's Guide to Complete Home Safety' (10 min.), National Film Board, 1986; 'The Old Lady's Camping Trip,' also National Film Board; or any locally produced video that refers to community rules.
People: Police Community Liaison Officer; Crossing Guard
Art supplies and materials.

Activities
1. Read *Tin Lizzie*. This book beautifully depicts the drastic changes in the North American way of life brought about by the advent of the mass-produced automobile. It also manages to capture some of the flavor of the love affair many people have with their cars! The book can be used in a variety of ways:

- to generate discussion. Focus on how changes brought about the need for new rules.
- to stimulate creative writing projects.
- to inspire artwork.
- as a resource for storydrama. (Children play the role of townspeople who are irate because of the chaos that the new cars are causing on their streets. What can they do about it?)

2. Mini Field Trip – a walk around the block. As the children walk around the block they record all the different traffic control indicators which they encounter. Back in the classroom, the class lists the indicators on the board and discusses their function.

3. Traffic Days in the Classroom – this activity can follow the storydrama. Children create a mini townscape in the classroom with murals, traffic signs, etc. They make hats and badges to indicate their roles as motorists, pedestrians, police officers, lawyers, judges, etc. Each child receives a unit of play money with which to pay traffic fines. The tone in the classroom should be one of fun and cooperation. Children who wish to challenge traffic tickets may make a court date when their case will be heard.

4. Guest Speaker: either a police officer or a crossing guard. Children prepare questions ahead of time. The issue of bicycle safety should be addressed here. Children can prepare a brief report on what they have learned, or make a list of bicycle safety rules to post in the classroom.

5. Show films about home and wilderness safety. They also can be used to generate creative writing, or visual or dramatic arts projects.

Evaluation

Children will be given a mark for participation, and individual projects in language and fine arts will be marked and recorded. As a culmination of this unit, Grade 3 children could be asked to write a short report on safety.

Topic #4: Rules Reflect Our Values – We Care About The Earth

General Remarks

This topic, like the last, also has potential for being expanded to form a unit on its own. It could be a part of a larger unit on ecology, or recycling, for example.

Objective

Children will understand that specific values underlie society's laws.

Intended Outcome

Children will become familiar with a few laws that govern the environment, such as municipal anti-littering bylaws and anti-pollution laws and will understand that these laws are a result of society's wish to preserve the earth.

Materials and Resources Tag board for a poster. A spokesperson from a community environmental group.

Activities Discussion of the earth's finite resources and the dangers of pollution. What are people attempting to do about the problem? Teachers outline a few laws that governments have made to address this issue. Arrange a visit by a resource person to give a presentation on recycling. Children brainstorm ways in which they can practise sound ecological behavior in the classroom.

Evaluation Children prepare a poster about an environmental concern.

Topic #5: Rules About Making Rules

Objective To introduce children to the qualities of a good rule or law.

Intended Outcome Children will be able to judge whether a rule is good or not using the criteria given in this topic.

Activities This topic requires some direct teaching of facts. The following will be introduced by the teacher and discussed with the children using hypothetical examples which contradict the criteria to illustrate the points. A good rule must:

- be clear and understandable (teacher may make up a classroom rule in gibberish or in a language unfamiliar to the students).

- be able to be followed (from now on you must only walk on the ceiling!).

- be enforceable (thoughts are not enforceable; 'from now on you may not think about food').

- be consistent with other rules in existence (teacher gives two rules which contradict one another).

- have a penalty for noncompliance (teacher tells a story about the day children arrived at school to find a new rule that did not allow them to sit down. At first they were dismayed, but they soon discovered that no one did anything about it if they disobeyed. Soon all the children resumed sitting to do their work, and although the rule existed it had no meaning because no one followed it. Discuss also the likelihood of such a rule ever coming into existence. Is it consistent with the school's values? Does it meet the needs of the students? the teacher?)

✏ be non-discriminatory (teacher makes one rule for brown-eyed people but informs the class that it does not apply to blue-eyed people. Is this a good rule? Why not? Introduce concept of justice.)

Resources   Book: *Strega Nona* by Tomie de Paola. Prentice Hall, 1975.

Evaluation   Make up three rules for either the class or school playground that meet the established criteria.

Topic #6 A Very Famous Rule – The Golden Rule

Objectives   The children will be introduced to an old concept of justice – one ought not to treat others any differently than one would want to be treated by others.

Intended Outcome   Children will learn what the term 'golden rule' refers to and will understand that it is a very ancient standard of behavior.

Resources   Book: *A Penny a Look* by Harve and Margo Zemach. New York: Farrar, Strauss, Giroux, 1971.

Activities   Read *A Penny A Look*. Ask children whether they think the outcome was fair. Explain that the 'hero' disobeyed a basic standard of behavior, namely the 'golden rule.' Explain and illustrate with examples. This book lends itself well to the use of a strategy called 'thinking boxes', in which children are given an opportunity to illustrate their comprehension and to make predictions about outcomes at several points in the story. There are also a lot of opportunities for artwork projects that arise out of reading this book. Children could draw the one-eyed people, or make signs advertising the amazing sight of the captive two-eyed men, etc.

Evaluation	Have children restate the golden rule in their own words and give an example of what they think it means.

Topic #7: People Are Different

Objective	To promote a climate of mutual acceptance and respect and to promote a sense that justice must be available to all.
Intended Outcome	Children will learn that good laws are fair and do not discriminate against people who are different.
Resources	Books: *The Big Orange Splot* by Daniel Manus Pinkwater. Hastings House, 1977. *Old Henry* by Joan W. Blos, illustrated by Stephen Gammell. New York: Wm. Morrow, 1987. *Angel Child, Dragon Child* by Michele Maria Surat, Illustrated by Vo-Dinh Mai. Milwaukee: Raintree, 1983. *Crow Boy* by Mitsu and Taro Yashima. Picture Puffins, Penguin Books Canada, 1955.
Activities	The first two books listed address the problem of deliberate non-conformity. In both books the neighborhood is disrupted by one resident who thinks differently about life than all the rest. The illustrative styles and the separate conclusions the books come to are vastly different. I would use them in conjunction with one another to stimulate discussion and to generate storydramas. In both instances, children could play the roles of neighbors who must address the problem of the non-conformist. Is it a crime to think differently? Do people have to think alike in order to get along? The next book, *Angel Child, Dragon Child*, sensitively introduces the concept of multi-culturalism. The story includes a conflict and a beautiful resolution brought about by the wisdom of the school principal who acts on his belief that prejudice and discrimination can be dispelled by people having an understanding of one another. I would use this book as a starting place for discussion of cultural diversity

and how it enriches society.

The last book, *Crow Boy*, deals with the most difficult issue: some people are different not because of their race, and not because they choose not to conform, but for some reason that is beyond their control they do not fit in with the group (social outcasts). The beauty and sensitivity with which this topic is handled make it a must for this section of study. Can rules address this problem? Can rules change people's attitudes? This introduces the limitations of rules and regulations. It is nearly impossible to regulate attitudes such as tolerance and kindness.

Evaluation

Art and writing projects which come out of the story-drama activities can be assessed to determine if children have grasped the concept of tolerance and respect for others. Both *Angel Child* and *Crow Boy* lend themselves to writing projects in which the child takes the role of one of the characters and describes their feelings. A reader's response log could also be used.

Additional Resources

Film: *Mary of Mile 18* based on the book of the same name by Ann Blades. National Film Board. Deals with family rules, and how a rule can be changed. *The Magic Quilt* (12 mins.), National Film Board. Deals with multiculturalism and conflict resolution.

Topic #8: We Make Our Own Rules

Objectives

Children will become participants in the regulation of their own lives and have a sense of ownership of rules.

Intended Outcome

Children will work together to draw up a few classroom rules (3-5) based on their expressed needs and values.

Materials

Chart paper and felt pens for a chart to be called, 'Our Civil Rights'.

Activities

Working together in small groups, children will come up with a list of possible problem areas in the classroom which could be addressed by rules. They will also draw up a list of values (2 or 3 would be enough) to keep in mind when making rules (see sample 'Our Civil Rights').

Working first in small groups, then as a whole class, children make up three to five rules to address the needs and values of the class. Children then refer to the criteria of a good rule (Topic #5) and test the rules they have made against these criteria, making changes where necessary. This learning experience lends itself well to the introduction of the democratic process. Class votes on which rules to include – a majority decision carries.

Rules are printed out on a poster and posted in the classroom. Class determines what the consequence of non-compliance will be, subject to veto by the teacher since children are often harsher than adults.

Additional Activities

1. Children design their own board game, making rules to address problems such as how are points scored, what happens, if anything, when two players land on the same square, how many people can play at once, etc.

2. Children invent a game with a method of scoring points and a system of rules as part of their physical education training.

OUR CIVIL RIGHTS

I have the right to be happy and to be treated with compassion in this room:

This means that no one will laugh at me or hurt my feelings.

I have the right to be myself in this room:

This means that no one will treat me unfairly because I am black or white, fat or thin, tall or short, boy or girl.

I have the right to be safe in this room:

This means that no one will hit me, kick me, push me, punch me or hurt me.

I have the right to hear and to be heard in this room:

This means that no one will yell, scream, shout or make loud noises.

I have the right to learn about myself in this room:

This means that I will be free to express my feelings and opinions without being interrupted or punished.

Topic #9: Rules Can Be Changed – We Amend Our Rules

Objectives	To promote the idea that rules are a response to society's needs and values and thus must be susceptible to amendment as needs and values change.
Intended Outcomes	Children will understand that rules are tools that people use to get along with one another and that people can control and alter them. They will be able to review the classroom rules they have made and make amendments, deletions or additions based on their review.
Resources	Poster of classroom rules and consequences.
Activities	Children meet in small groups to discuss the classroom rules. Are they necessary? Are they effective in addressing the problems they were meant to address? Are the consequences fair and effective? etc. What kind of changes would children like to see in the rules, and why? Individually, children fill out a classroom rule report card (see sample). Report cards are tallied and results indicate which rules, if any, need amendment. Children vote on amendments.

Classroom Rule Report Card

Rule #1 (print the rule here)

Do we need this rule? If yes, why do you think so?

If you think we should keep this rule, does it need to be changed?
Give your suggestion for how this rule should be changed

Rule #2 (Continue as above for each of the classroom rules)

References and Resources

A Resource Guide to Assist Lawyers and Law Students for Participation in Kindergarten though Eighth Grade Law-Related Classrooms. (1981). Washington, D.C.: Phi Alpha Delta Law Fraternity International, Juvenile Justice Office.

Audio-Visual and Publications Catalogues. Published each year by the Legal Services Society of British Columbia.

Educating for Citizenship (Vol. 1). (1982). Rockville, MD: Aspen Law-Related Education Series, Aspen Systems Corp.

Lawmaking: Law in Action Series, 2nd edition for teachers: (1980). Riekes-Ackerly. *Lessons in Law for Young People*. St. Paul: West Publishing Co.

CHAPTER 8
Experiencing Law Through Games and Simulations

Ruth Yates

Because law is not taught in public schools as a discrete discipline, teachers who want to include legal concepts in their lessons must find ways of integrating them into mainstream subjects. There are many opportunities in the classroom to teach about the law, how it is created, what social purposes it serves and how it is enforced without actually presenting a lesson on the law.

Over the years of working with teachers who teach law or legal concepts in elementary and secondary classes, we have collected many helpful teaching ideas, lesson resources and unit plans and we thought it might be helpful to include some of them here to serve primarily as models that can be adapted for use in any classroom. The mock trial is a strategy familiar to many teachers; for others who may not have attempted one because of its seeming complexity, we have provided a simple outline to help you through the process that will give students a better understanding of the judicial process. Children like to play games that simulate real life and so we have included a simulation activity based on the ideas of law-making, representative government, interest groups and negotiation. The reasoning and decision-making skills that are important elements in the legal system are skills that we want children to acquire. Providing children opportunities to practise them is one of the objectives of another exercise that we have included, called the Justice Circle, which simulates an alternative method of resolving legal problems.

Simulation Activities
Mock Trials

A mock trial is a simulation activity in which students undertake to stage a trial in their classroom or in a courtroom. They range from the prosecution of a fictional character to the re-enactment of an actual trial. They can be acted out from a prepared script or can rely on the research and presentations of students who assume the roles of accused, victim, witnesses, defence and prosecution counsel, judges and court officers. Mock trials can provide a valuable means of introducing students to legal concepts and courtroom procedure and can be undertaken in almost any classroom from the second grade on. The complexity of the undertaking is limited only by the energy and enthusiasm of the teacher and students. Mock trial kits designed for different age groups are available and may be helpful for a class attempting their first mock trial, but enough information follows to allow you to experiment with one in your classroom. After the first experience you will look for any opportunity to create your own mock trial and doing so will yield great benefits for your students.

The first step in deciding to do a mock trial is determining the educational goals that it will achieve. It should be connected to a learning unit in either language arts or social studies or, as we demonstrate in Chapter 10, even in science. These are some of the learning outcomes that have been developed by teachers who have used mock trials in their classes:

A mock trial

- develops student enthusiasm for the law;

- enables students to learn legal principles first-hand;

- motivates students to get more involved with curricular material;

- develops students' empathy for those involved in the criminal justice system;

- gives students an opportunity to appreciate the reasons for procedure and rules of evidence;

- helps teach cooperation, communication, clarification, critical thinking and listening skills;

- may result in attitudinal change, greater confidence in dealing with adversity, more openness to new experiences and new willingness to modify position.

The elements required for a mock criminal trial are an incident in which a crime is committed, an accused person, a victim and witnesses to the criminal act. If the focus of the unit to be taught is based on a work of fiction, perhaps the characters and incident could become the basis of a mock trial. If it is a social studies class and the topic is historical in nature, perhaps research could be done on an actual incident and a trial could be re-enacted based on the historical characters and events. It is also possible to invent characters who might have participated in an otherwise factual historical event. Whether creating the trial from fictional or real characters and events, the procedure is the same and can be modified to suit the needs of the class.

Step 1 – Setting the Scene

Identify and describe the scene in which the crime is committed, providing sufficient background information for the students to be able to determine the facts of the case. Determine who the victim is, what the circumstances are and what injuries have been suffered. The teacher may decide to have students dramatize the crime scene as a way of setting the stage for the trial. Identify the likely perpetrator and determine what criminal charge is going to be laid against the offender. Assume that all required pre-trial processes have been conducted and the accused has been given a trial date.

Step 2 – Preparing for Trial

Select a team of three students to take on the role of the prosecution. Another team of three students will become the defence counsel. The two teams familiarize themselves with the known facts and interview the defendant and any witnesses to the incident.

Step 3 – Getting the Facts

Select three students to act as witnesses for the prosecution, and three others as witnesses for the defence. Each should be given a role card that describes what they saw or what they know about the defendant or the victim. The witnesses must know about the incident and be able to answer lawyers' questions about what they saw relevant to the offence or what they know about the accused or the victim. Experts in a particular crime (forensic scientists), or illness (medical professionals) may be called to testify at the trial even if they did not witness the crime. They should conduct their own research to find out as much as they can about the nature of the crime and the capacity of the accused to commit the crime.

The lawyers prepare questions to ask witnesses on the stand. Each team prepares opening and closing statements designed to convince the judge and jury that the accused is either guilty or innocent of the crime with which he or she has been charged.

Step 4 – Staging the Trial

Select a person to be the judge and call eight, ten or twelve students to be members of the jury. A court clerk, court reporter and sheriff round out the personnel of the courtroom and each should receive the outline of trial procedures to help them prepare for their role.

Allow class time for students to meet in their teams, interview witnesses and prepare their courtroom strategies. If it is not possible to arrange to have the mock trial staged in a regular courtroom, arrange the classroom furniture to resemble a courtroom and borrow legal gowns for the judge and lawyers to wear. Costuming for participants enhances the dramatic elements of the simulation and encourages students to take their roles seriously. Gowns can usually be borrowed from the local courthouse.

Diagram of Courtroom and Court Proceedings

The diagram of the Courtroom, and the Court Proceedings on the following pages have been provided by:

Diagram: Legal Services Society of B.C. (1987). *Learning Law Through Mock Trials.*

Court Proceedings: British Columbia Law Courts Education Society Legal Safari (Part 3) *Adventures in Justice.*

Step 5 – Trying the Case

Court Proceedings:

Sheriff:	All rise, this Court is now in session. His/her Honor Judge _____ presiding. (Everyone remains standing until the Judge tells them to be seated.)
Judge:	You may be seated
Court Clerk:	The case of the Queen versus _____.
Judge:	Thank you. Are all parties present?
Crown:	(stands and addresses the Judge) Yes, Your Honor. I am _____ and these are my learned friends _____ and _____. We are acting on behalf of the Crown.
Defence:	(stands and addresses the Judge) Yes, Your Honor. I am _____ and these are my learned friends _____ and _____. We are acting on behalf of the accused.
Judge:	Thank you. (To court clerk) Please read the charge. (Judge addresses the accused) Please rise to hear the charge. (The accused, the defence lawyers and the Court Clerk rise.)
Court Clerk:	_____, you are charged with _____ on (date) at (time) and (place). How do you plead?
Accused:	Not guilty.
Court Clerk:	Your Honor, the accused pleads "not guilty."
Judge:	(Addresses the Crown) Please proceed with your case. [The judge calls for opening statements from the prosecution This is a two- or three-minute review of the facts of the case and suggests why the accused is guilty of the crime.]

The Setting

The diagram below shows the lay-out of a criminal courtroom.

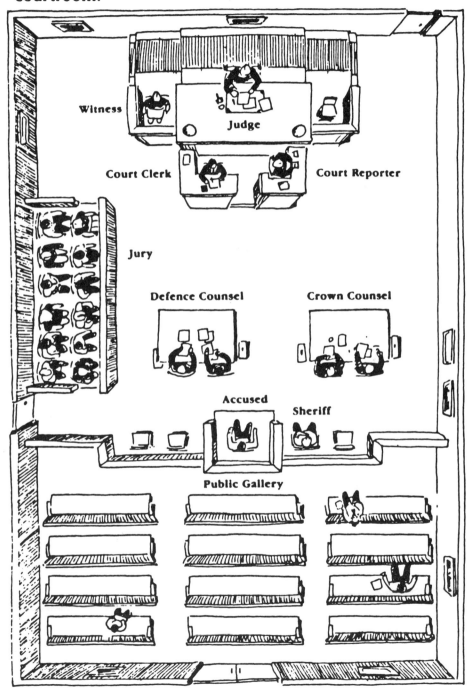

Crown:	(Opening Statement) . . . We now wish to call our first witness, _____.
Court Clerk:	(To witness) Take the Bible in your right hand. Do you swear to tell the truth, the whole truth and nothing but the truth, so help you God?
Witness No. 1:	I do.
	(Crown proceeds with their questions.)
Judge:	Does the Defence wish to cross-examine this witness?
Defence:	Yes, Your Honor. (Stands and questions Crown Witness Number 1.)
	(This procedure follows for each Crown witness.)
Judge:	(To the Crown) Do you wish to call any more witnesses?
Crown:	No, Your Honor. We rest our case.
Judge:	(To Defence) Would the Defence please begin.
Defence:	(Opening Statement and informs the Court which witnesses will be called for the Defence)
Court Clerk:	(Calls the witnesses in turn, swearing each of them in as before. Defence conducts its examination and each witness may be cross-examined by the Crown)
Defence:	(Completes its case) We rest our case, Your Honor.
Judge:	(Invites Defence to begin their Closing Statement. This is a brief summary of the major points brought forward by the witnesses for the defence.)
Defence:	(Closing Statement to Jury.)
Judge:	(Invites the Crown to give their Closing Statement.)
Crown:	(Closing Statement to Jury. This is a brief summary of the major points brought forward by the Crown's witnesses)
Judge:	(Instructs the Jury.)
	(Jury leaves to decide on their verdict. It is more interesting for the audience if the jury deliberates in their presence.)
	(Jury returns.)
Judge:	Ladies and gentlemen of the jury, have you reached your verdict?
Jury Foreman:	Yes, Your Honor, on the charge of _____ we find the accused (guilty/not guilty).
	(The Judge lets the accused go free if the verdict is not guilty. If the verdict is guilty . . . .)
Judge:	Would the Crown please speak to the Sentence.

Crown:	(The Crown will be prepared to suggest a suitable Sentence, in their opinion.)
Judge:	Thank you. Would the Defence please speak to the Sentence.
Defence:	(The Defence will be prepared to suggest a suitable Sentence, in their opinion.)
Judge:	(Sentences the accused) This court is now adjourned.
Court Clerk:	All rise, this court is now adjourned. (Everyone stands while the Judge leaves the courtroom.)

Step 6 – Debriefing

It is important to hold a debriefing session after the trial. Ask students how they felt in their various roles. Did the testimony at trial give them a different perspective about the crime, the offender or the victim? Was the process fair? Did all the information come out? Ask them about what they have learned about the justice system and how it has affected their attitudes about the law. What do lawyers have to know before they can properly prosecute or defend a person accused of a crime? Question them about the suitability of the verdict and the difficulties of judging and sentencing an accused. Try to determine if the students think the problem could have been solved any other way.

Simulation Games

The use of simulation games in the classroom helps students in three major areas. Participants:

- improve their skills at analyzing and making judgments in a situation, and can experience immediate consequences.

- gain insight into their own behavior and develop sensitivity to the behavior of others.

- practice and refine skills in dealing effectively with one another.

Simulation games can take many forms and there are numerous examples in published curriculum materials that can be used as models for games teachers may develop on their own. We are including one sample here that might be suitable for students from Grades 5 to 7.

There has been a lot of discussion in the recent past about Canada's Constitution and how it should be changed. Students will realize that the process of changing the constitution is a very complex one and requires a lot of debate, negotiation and compromise. They should understand that most of our laws are made by our representatives in the legislature of the provinces and in the federal parliament. If citizens want to participate in the rule-making process they must understand the principle of representation. The Constitution Game is designed to give children a sense of what it means to represent the interests of a group and helps them to understand the different characteristics that make a group of people distinctive. Laws should protect the rights of individuals but they must also order society and satisfy the needs of particular groups, and participants in this game will get a sense of the frustration of trying to respond to their own desires as well as what is best for their region or their country.

Constitution Game

Define what a constitution is by relating it to classroom rules. (A constitution is to a country what class rules are to a class.)

Why do we need a constitution? (To give order to the country, to protect its citizens, to organize society and enable it to progress in a peaceful and just way.)

Who makes the rules? (The citizens or their representatives in government.)

How long does it take to make rules? (Depends on how many people are involved and how complex the issues are.)

How does it happen? (Through discussion, debate, negotiation and compromise.)

How was it done in Canada? (Because Canada started out as a colony of Great Britain, an old nation that had already learned to live according to democracy, Canada adopted many rules that had worked in Britain. After Canada had some practice being a nation, we decided to keep some of the British rules but not bother with the rest and to create some new rules of our own.)

The idea of this game is to make some social changes by deciding which rules we would all want to live by, which rules need to be removed, changed or added. People create rules for their own small groups to live by whether the group is a family, a school, a business or a community. For the rules that govern the whole country, they elect representatives or members of parliament to make the rules for them. Citizens give their representatives instructions and encouragement but once they go to parliament, citizens are stuck with their decisions at least until the next election.

Rules are based on what we value or think is important. In this game each student will become the representative of a particular group of people. The groups are made up of people who live in a certain areas like the North, the Maritimes or the Prairies. They are also made up of people who have distinctive characteristics. That is, they all come from a certain country, or they all speak a certain language, or they are all women, or all train engineers. Every group has some special interests that they want other groups to recognize and respect. Each student is given a role card which will tell them what group they are going to represent. Once a student knows who they are they will look for other representatives that they have something in common with. Nothing gets done if we have to do it all by ourselves, so it is always best to team up with people who share our interests and beliefs and who want and need the same things we do. The first area of common interest is the region of the country that the people live in. People with role cards the same color are from the same region of the country. So participants' first task is to find the people who live in the same area and then to find out what the other people in that area are interested in.

These are some of the questions students should try to answer by studying their role cards.

1. Where do we live?

2. What languages do we speak?

3. What different groups live in our region?

4. What kind of work do we do?

5. What is the most important thing in our lives?

Then each regional group should decide the three most important rules that they would like to have in their country. Rules can be chosen from a list that is handed out to the group.

After your group has written the three most important rules on a piece of paper, the person in the group with a dark circle on their role card will become the representative for the group in the national parliament. The spokesperson from each group will take the three rules their group has selected and attend the national meeting where they will work together to come up with a list of 12 rules from all the ones that each group has selected. While the representatives are meeting, the rest of their group will try to find people in other groups who have a symbol on their role cards that is the same as their own. Locate other individuals with the same symbols on their role cards; they should sit together and discuss their interests and concerns and determine what they have in common with one another. Individuals must then decide if they will vote in support of their regional group representatives or if they will vote to support their special interest group.

The representatives will then call a general meeting and present the 12 final rules that they have agreed upon. These rules should be written on the blackboard where everyone can see them. Then begins the voting process. Each spokesperson has five affirmative votes on each of three rules (because they represent the original groups). The teacher should keep track of the voting on the blackboard according to the attached chart. The representatives' votes should be recorded on the chart first, at the conclusion of their meeting, and then voting should be opened up to the rest of the participants. Each of the other players has one affirmative vote on each of three rules, and one negative vote on each of three others, but if they can persuade four other people to vote the same way they do, they have enough power to neutralize a representative's vote if they vote against the rule, or if they vote for the rule, it will be enough to get it passed. (Ten votes are required to make a rule a law.)

At the end of the activity, there should be 9 laws that form the constitution of the new Canada. Is everyone satisfied with the final list of rules? Are they enough to run a country by? What is missing? How would you change any of these rules? How do your rules for a nation compare with your classroom rules?

Suggested Rules

1. Citizens have the right not to be harmed or injured by others.
2. Citizens have the right to speak freely even when they are critical of the government and disrespectful of other people.
3. Citizens have the right to elect representatives to the government.
4. Citizens have the right to a decent job with a fair wage.
5. Citizens have the right to live where they want and to travel freely in Canada and the United States.
6. The government has the right to tax the people to pay the costs of governing.
7. All people should be treated equally.
8. All people have the right to post-secondary education.
9. All people have the right to medical care.
10. All people have the right to legal assistance.
11. Everyone has the right to breathe clean air and drink clean water.
12. Everyone should be able to speak and get government services in the language of their choice.
13. Everyone should be able to hunt animals, catch fish, cut trees or find minerals wherever they want to.
14. Everyone has the right to own property and be protected from interference from others.
15. Citizens who can't find work or who live in poor areas should get extra money from the government.
16. Native people should have the right to govern themselves.
17. Women should earn the same as men for the same job.
18. Day-care should be available to all children.
19. Everyone should be able to practice whatever religion they want.
20. Everyone has the right to be treated fairly under the law.

Role Cards

Requires five 8 1/2- by 11-inch colored sheets which can be cut into six squares, with each square containing a description of a person who lives in the region. The sheets are cut and distributed to class members.

Green – West Coast & Yukon; Red – Prairies & N.W.T.; Yellow – Ontario; Blue – Quebec; White – Maritimes

Ontario – Yellow Paper

● ○1. You live in a small town in Ontario. You work in a mine and like to hunt and fish on the weekends. You have a young family and hardly make enough money to pay the mortgage and buy food.	▼4. You and your family have been living in Ontario for five generations. You think that schools, businesses and governments should only be conducted in English because that would save a lot of money and people would all be treated the same.
■2. You live in a big city in Southern Ontario. You work in a steel plant and like to watch football and hockey games on the weekends. You make good money but it costs more than you earn to send your kids to university.	◆5. You are a Native person living on a reservation in Northern Ontario. You live in poverty and the government has treated your people very badly over the years. You cannot find work and your kids are having trouble in school.
▲3. You are a French-speaking resident of Ontario and are sending your kids to separate schools where they can be educated in French and that is costing you a lot of money and you don't think its fair that you should have to pay extra for their education.	▶6. You are a woman living in Ontario and have not been able to work full-time for a decent wage partly because jobs are scarce and especially because you can't get good day-care for your kids.

Quebec – Blue Paper

○1. You work for a hydro-electric power company in Northern Quebec. There are a lot of complaints about the damage hydro projects do to the environment because of flooding, but you like your job and living in a small community and you don't want the power company to shut down even if it is causing environmental problems.

● ■2. You work for a computer software company in Montreal. You have a university education and think that your kids should go to university too. But they have to go out of Quebec to get the special kind of training they need.

▲3. You are a French-speaking Quebecer who thinks that Quebec should separate from the rest of Canada. You think that English-speaking Canadians control the country and that French-speaking Canadians do not have the same opportunities for education and work and that the province could do better on its own.

▼4. You are an English-speaking resident of Quebec and are afraid that if Quebec separates, the company you work for will move to Toronto. You'd rather live in Quebec because you like the culture, but there may not be many opportunities for you work here if the English companies move.

◆5. You are a Native person living near Montreal. You are not very happy with the way the Quebec Government has been treating Natives. You have the opportunity to work just across the border in New York State but you have trouble crossing back and forth across the border because of government regulations.

▶6. You are a French-speaking woman in Quebec and feel that women are not treated fairly by the law and courts in Quebec and that you don't have equal access to work that pays fair wages.

Maritimes – White Paper

○1. You are a fisherman living in Newfoundland and have not been able to work because of the shortage of fish. Government regulations have hurt the industry and now you must rely on welfare to support your family. Life is hard but you don't want to move away from the Rock because it has been your family's home for more than a century.

▼4. You live in Prince Edward Island and have always had a good living on your family farm. You like the quiet life of the Island and are not very happy with the new bridge that connects the Island to the mainland. You are afraid it will bring a lot of strangers and you will lose the happy isolation of your home.

■2. You are a teacher in Nova Scotia and are worried because so many young people are leaving the province to find work in Ontario. You would like your children to stay in Nova Scotia, but you know that there aren't very many opportunities for them here.

◆5. You are a Native person living in the Maritimes. You like to hunt and fish but also need a steady job to support your family. You are tired of government support and want your children to grow up to be independent and productive.

● ▲3. You are a French-speaking person in New Brunswick and are worried what will happen if Quebec decides to separate. Will there still be French schools for your children to attend and will you be able to get government services in French?

▶6. You have been a traditional housewife who would now like to start a career but know that you need to get some training before that is possible. There aren't many opportunities for women to get that in small-town Nova Scotia and you need a government incentive program to help you accomplish your goals.

Prairies – Red Paper

○1. You are a Saskatchewan wheat farmer whose family has lived on the land for generations. But now that machinery is so expensive and the price of wheat is so low, it is getting harder to make the farm self-sustaining. You need help and want the government to give extra support to Prairie grain farmers.

● ▼4. You are a librarian in Regina and think that Canada has an important history and heritage that needs to be preserved. A lot of it happened in the Prairies but because of changes in rural and farm life, many of the residents are giving up and moving away. You want to do something to help them stay.

■2. You work for a fibre-optics manufacturing plant in Winnipeg. It's a high-tech job and you had to get specialized training in Toronto in order to get it. You hope your children will be able to live nearby but the opportunities for training just aren't available in Manitoba.

◆5. You are a Native person living in a small town in Southern Alberta. It has not been an easy life because there is still a lot of prejudice against Native people here. You want the opportunity to organize your community to serve its own needs.

▲3. You are a second-generation Ukrainian living in Western Manitoba on a farm your parents homesteaded 60 years ago. You would like your children to learn the culture and language of your parents but you are afraid that in the public schools there are no opportunities for that to happen.

◗6. You are a farm wife who has worked hard on the family farm, but now you are separating from your husband and you find that you have no claim on the assets of the farm because they are all in your husband's name. You have no other way to support yourself and want fair treatment in the divorce settlement.

West Coast – Green Paper

○1. You are a logger from Vancouver Island and your job is threatened by environmentalists who want to preserve the whole place as parkland. You have a family to take care of and you think there is room for both parks and logging operations and you want the government to make it possible to use more responsible logging practices.

▼4. You moved to B.C. from back East 25 years ago when it was still a small-town kind of place. It has grown fast and most of the new people are immigrants from Asia. They seem to be taking all the good jobs, buying up all the property and filling up most of the schools, so you wonder if the government shouldn't change its immigration policies.

■2. You are a furniture store owner in a big city in B.C. Because of cross-border shopping, cut-rate department stores and huge malls, your business is in trouble. It doesn't help that taxes are so high that people aren't buying as much as they used to. You need a break and something to encourage people to support local retailers.

●◆5. You are a Native person living in Vancouver. You left your parents' home because there was no work on the reserve. It is hard to find a job in the city and you hate living there. You want the freedom of living closer to nature but there is no way to survive out there.

▲3. You are a recent immigrant from Asia and your children must learn to speak English but the schools are so crowded and underfunded that they don't have a fighting chance. You want them to have opportunities you didn't have and you are willing to work hard but need a living wage to survive.

◗6. You are a young woman lawyer who wants a successful career but you also want to have a family and there seems no way to have both. To succeed as a lawyer you have to spend endless hours at the office and compete for clients and work. In such a competitive world it is almost impossible to take time out for family life.

Constitution Game – Voting Chart

Regions	Maritimes	Quebec	Ontario	Prairies	West Coast	PEOPLE	TOTAL
LAWS							
1						+ —	
2						+ —	
3						+ —	
4						+ —	
5						+ —	
6						+ —	
7						+ —	
8						+ —	
9						+ —	
10						+ —	
11						+ —	
12						+ —	

When the group has come up with a final list of rules, the teacher should point out that successful laws must address three facets of people's lives – as individual people, as part of a group or region, and finally as citizens of a nation. The class could categorize the laws they have made in terms of their fitting into these three categories. Determine whether the rules the class has come up with satisfy all three components and discuss what other rules are actually in the constitution that make national life possible.

Role-Play Activity

A role-play activity that encourages children to think about the justice system is a simulation based on a new strategy being used by the Canadian justice system to address some of the problems in Canada's First Nations communities. Our legal system has traditionally not responded well to the difficulties faced by First Nations people. Now the judicial system is beginning to turn to ancient traditions and practices of the Native people themselves as a way of solving problems that arise when Native people come into conflict with Canadian law.

This simulation, called Justice Circle, is an activity that can involve the entire class and be based on any number of offenses that may occur in the school or in the local community. The first step is to identify an offence that is a common problem in your school or neighborhood. For the purposes of this example, we will undertake to solve a problem of vandalism at the school.

Step 1 – Setting the Scene

There has been a rash of acts of vandalism on the school property in recent weeks. The damage usually occurs after everyone has left for the day and involves broken windows, damaged door locks where someone has used a crowbar or some other instrument to try to get into the school, and garbage cans being overturned and their contents spread around the playground. The problem has been causing concern to everyone at the school. The principal is concerned because of the cost and problem of getting doors and windows repaired. The students dislike the mess in their playing area. Everyone is very relieved when a Grade 6 student is finally caught in the act by a teacher. Now everyone wonders what should be done to punish the offender, and to prevent something like this from happening again. The school authorities don't want to lay charges and turn the case over to the police so they decide to deal with it another way, by organizing a justice circle.

Step 2 – Selecting Participants for the Justice Circle

After describing the above scenario for your students, tell them that they are going to be the players in the Justice Circle that has been set up by the principal. A student will act as the young offender and will have one student assigned as a defence counsel who will protect the rights of the person accused of the offense. Other students will play the parts of the offender's parents, guardians or siblings and a social worker who has been assigned to work with the family. One student will be a police officer who has been called in to offer advice and talk about the other ways the problem might be dealt with in the courts. Another student can take on the role of the school principal and several others might be the teachers of the offending student. Students can also act as friends of the offender. After assigning the roles, break the class up into smaller groups, made up of family members, school and community workers, where they can share their ideas about the offense, the offender and what should be done. The person assigned to defend the offender should circulate among the three groups to get a feeling for everyone's opinion about the case. Remind students to discuss the situation from the point of view of the person they are role-playing. Students should be instructed to write on a 8 by 5 card the following information:

Name:

➥ What is your relationship to the offender?

➥ What do you know about the offender?

➥ How have you been hurt by the offense?

➥ What do you think should be done about it?

Students should also think about how they would answer the following questions:

➥ What extenuating circumstances affect this case?

➥ Have there been other problems with the student in the past?

➥ Is there trouble at home?

➥ How has he or she been doing in school?

➥ What's best for the offender?

➥ How can the school be compensated for the damage that has been done? How can this problem be prevented in the future?

Step 3 – Creating the Circle

When the groups have shared their feelings and ideas and the individuals have filled out their role cards, it is time to tell the class how a Justice Circle works. Clear a large area in the centre of a classroom or the gym and have the students sit in a large circle that includes all participants. The teacher should be the circle leader, sitting at the head of the circle and holding a talking stick and the others should be seated in the order in which they will speak. The circle leader states the purpose of the gathering, which is to decide what should be done about the person caught damaging school property. Each of the people in the circle have a special interest and each are then given an opportunity to introduce themselves and tell about their relationship to the offender. The talking stick is passed to each participant as they speak in turn, beginning with the counsel for the offender and followed by the people closest to him or her. This group is followed by the teachers who have been involved with the student and then the principal, who tells about the damage caused to the school. The final people to report are the social worker and the police officer.

Step 4 – Solving the Problem

When everyone in the circle has had an opportunity to speak, the circle leader asks one person from each group (family, school, community) to summarize the feelings of their group and suggest a solution. The circle leader reviews the possible solutions and asks the group to come to a consensus. When a solution is reached the circle leader affirms the decision and sets out the action to be taken against the offender. As much as possible the consequences should look to returning the offender to the community, repairing and reimbursing the school for the damages and restoring the confidence of the students and teachers at the school.

Step 5 – Debriefing

When the Justice Circle has finished its work, be sure to talk to students about the experience, giving them time to come out of their roles and to think about how their perspective on an act changes when they are the offender, the victim or someone close to either. Would this be a better way to solve problems than in a traditional court where people who care about the offender are not given a chance to be heard? What are the advantages and disadvantages?

Case Study Carousel

This relatively simple exercise, based loosely on the case study method used for older students, will give younger children an opportunity to look at a problem that would normally be solved in the courts, and allow them to separate out the important parts of the case and try to resolve it. For this exercise you may use situations that have occurred in the classroom or school where someone's personal property or rights have been interfered with or you might choose to use cases that have been tried in court or that are currently being reported in the newspaper. You may use incidents related in stories that the class has studied. Select four scenarios or cases, write them up briefly and have each one of them posted at a different location in the room along with four charts with the following headings:

1. Complaint or Problem

2. Victim's Position

3. Offender's Position

4. Judge's Decision

Divide the class into four groups sending one group to each station. The group at each station reads the scenario and then fills out the first chart. The groups then move on to the next station, read the scenario and fill out the second chart. The rotation continues until all charts have been filled out. The last group at each station then reports on the case that they have made the decision on and the class discusses the outcome. Opinions will differ because of the perspective each group has on the case and discussion may follow on the appropriateness of the decisions made in each case.

CHAPTER 9
Facing an Issue Through Critical Thinking and Decision-Making in Social Studies

Shelby L. Sheppard

Legal concepts are implicit in the content of many subject areas of contemporary curricula; it is often simply a matter of recognizing and bringing them to the attention of our students and by doing so we can transform their understanding and heighten their appreciation of the existing course content.

A central idea within law-related education is the ease with which important legal concepts and procedures may be adapted and integrated into existing course content. The benefits of raising students' awareness of legal concepts and procedures are twofold. First, as we live in a "legal-rational" society (governed by the rule of law), awareness of *what this means* is an important part of our students' education. Second, by bringing legal concepts and procedures to the attention of students, we can bring the course content to life with interesting new approaches to existing curricula. The learning unit presented here is one that I taught in a Grade 5 classroom and is only one example of how teachers may add a significant element to an existing program, and by so doing, transform their students' understanding.

Background Information

The Grade 5 Social Studies program in British Columbia focuses on several central and interrelated themes in Canadian history including fur trading, gold mining and the building of the Canadian Pacific Railway (C.P.R.). In dealing with this material I followed suggestions from a book by Kieran Egan called *Teaching As Story-Telling* (1987). Egan suggests that teachers provide learning experiences from *within* a historical and geographical framework. The relationships between the themes can be made meaningful for children if they become "actors" in the course content and "live" the experiences of Canadian history.

In my classroom each theme was illustrated and enhanced by a changing class mural which covered an entire wall from floor to ceiling. The mural in this unit was a topographical background of Canada (See Figure 1). Students decided what the mural should portray (in each theme), outlined areas in chalk, labelled and signed them to indicate their responsibility for the particular representation. Throughout the unit they worked on "bringing their environment to life." By the end of the theme, the mural was a complete representation of the *students' view of the context*. In addition, the students chose characters from the historical context, drew life-sized head and shoulder portraits, and adopted the persona (when appropriate) of their characters. The portraits were displayed around the room above the chalkboards and appeared to "look down" at the class. In some cases, whole groups of students adopted the persona of a single character for purposes of an activity (e.g., Chief Crowfoot, Inspector Steele of the N.W.M.P.).

The theme was further enhanced by filling the room with theme-related literature, audio-visual materials (see specific lessons) and the projects completed by the students. In addition, students brought in theme-related literature and artifacts from their homes and the community. The students' interest and growing awareness led to their finding resource people who they invited to the class for presentations and discussion (e.g., a railway engineer who happened to be a history "buff," a police officer who was interviewed by a student for a theme project, etc.).

Activities within the Social Studies themes included "mime" presentations and appropriate ukulele-accompanied songs. (Note – students often composed music and/or lyrics from creative writing activities.) The presentations were videotaped and titled with computer-generated graphics done by the students. The program began each morning (Monday through Thursday) at 8:55 a.m. and ran until recess at 10:15 a.m.. Activities were also carried on at other times of the day, as desired. Each day usually began with a "shared reading" activity. A student in each of the 5 groups volunteered to "share" for the following day, one of: (i) a passage from the related literature in the room; (ii) his/her journal entry from the day before; and (iii) theme-related literature brought from home or the public library. The student-pre-senter introduced his or her selection by explaining why it was chosen, read the selection to the group and conducted a discussion of the material.

A variation of this activity is to have all students in the group share similar journal entries. Each group then selects a representative to present to the whole class. In this way, the class develops an understanding of the writing styles and subject areas that appeal to their peers. Needless to say, the quality and originality of the students' writing are greatly enhanced by this type of activity. All students are expected to participate but in our class they did so with such enthusiasm that we rotated, giving everyone the opportunity to "share."

It is within this broader context then, that the law-related unit, "Facing an Issue," occurred. Guidelines for the unit were set by the Grade 5 Social Studies program based on the text *Canada: Building Our Nation*, particularly Chapter 9: "Facing an Issue at Blackfoot Crossing." It should be remembered that this is a sample of what might be done in a history unit; the text references and even the event itself can be adapted by the teacher to suit the needs of the course and text materials that are available.

Critical Thinking and Decision-Making:

In our "legal-rational" society we expect our leaders to make good decisions which are based on supporting reasons. The reasons why a leader may judge that it is best to do "this" rather than "that" are not chosen at random, nor are they simply the leader's personal opinions about what is best. The reasons that a leader gives to support a decision are the result of thoughtful deliberation and consideration of such things as the positive and negative consequences and the long-term and short-term implications of a particular action. They participate in the reasoning exercise we call "thinking critically."

In the chapter "Building the C.P.R.," in *Canada: Building Our Nation*, the Blackfoot chief, Crowfoot, was required to make an important decision, namely, whether or not to allow the railway access to previously-designated reservation lands. The decision was not an easy one as Crowfoot had to consider conflicting views among his own people in addition to both the benefits and potential problems that might result should he allow the railroad access. Crowfoot's decision provided an excellent opportunity for my Grade 5 students to "experience" a leader's sense of responsibility to his people and to recognize what it means to "face an issue" and make a decision.

The important elements seemed to be:

(1) to assess an issue and recognize the available options;

(2) to recognize the consequences and implications of each option;

(3) to weigh the consequences and implications carefully; and

(4) to render a decision and articulate the reasons supporting it.

The following lessons were designed to develop student awareness of these elements and to contrast them with the students' natural tendencies to make decisions based on satisfying their personal preferences, peer group pressure, popular opinions and what is often misleading or inaccurate information.

The unit was highly successful in terms of achieving the desired goals. As the students became aware of the legal concepts and procedures through role-playing, it became evident that they had begun to understand and accept their character's responsibility for rendering a thoughtful decision. Significantly, many students changed their position on the decision several times throughout the course of the unit. Each change in position represented a visible transformation of the student's understanding of the issue. The original Social Studies program lost nothing due to the addition of the law-related elements. Rather, the new lessons made it significantly more meaningful and added a new dimension to the students' understanding of the historical events.

The educational value of the notion of thinking critically in order to arrive at thoughtful, reasoned decisions was evident both during the unit and long after the class had moved on to other activities. The students demonstrated their new understanding in class discussions, in written assignments and in the kinds of critical questions that they posed for teachers and their peers. Clearly, "facing an issue" was instrumental in transforming the way these students viewed their world and would undertake responsibilities as citizens in our society.

FIGURE 1: CLASS MURAL – BUILDING THE C.P.R.

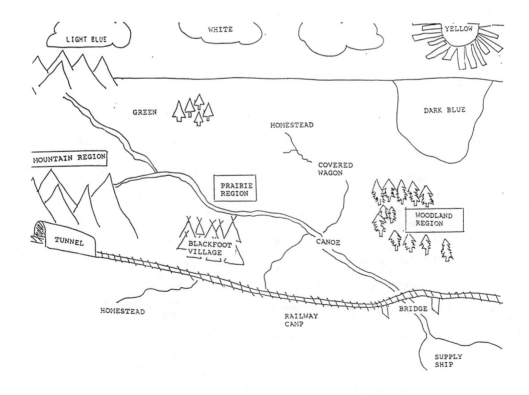

Lesson #1: Historical Context

Historical Context

1. The people involved in the incident include: the Blackfoot tribe, Chief Crowfoot, a government agent, a railway grading crew, Father Albert Lacombe, Edgar Dewdney (Lieutenant-Governor), members of the North West Mounted Police and Commissioner Irvine.

2. The time and place of the confrontation is May 1883 at Blackfoot Crossing near Fort Calgary.

Law-related Concepts

1. The treaty signed by Chief Crowfoot in 1877 gave the Blackfoot the *right* to land reserved for their use only. The Canadian government kept the *right* to build roads through the reserve.

2. Chief Crowfoot had the *responsibility* to make decisions on behalf of his people.

3. The treaty between the Blackfoot and the Canadian Government was a *legal document*.

4. The treaty contained promises made by both groups. The Blackfoot agreed to give up land for settlers and in return the government promised to provide food to the Blackfoot people.

Related Reading

Chapter 9 – *Canada: Building Our Nation* (Prentice-Hall) (or text of your choosing)

Activities

1. Groups read Chapter to find answer to the following questions:

Group 1 –   Who were the Blackfoot and where did they live?

Group 2 –   What was the treaty about? What concerns did the Blackfoot have? What concerns did the government have?

Group 3 –   What problems were caused by the survey crew? Why was Chief Crowfoot concerned?

Group 4 –   What was the role of Father Lacombe in the issue? How did he propose to solve the problem?

Group 5 –   What interests did Edgar Dewdney and Commissioner Irvine have in the issue? What suggestions did they offer?

2. Group discussion of reading to answer the questions.

3. Group representatives present results of their exercise to class.

4. Students write individual journal entries in the role of the character they have adopted responding to the question "What was Chief Crowfoot's Problem?"

Skills

1. Locating information from text

2. Identifying main ideas

3. Oral communication – discussing information

4. Decision-making – synthesizing information

5. Working towards consensus – group presentation

Lesson #2: The Issue

Thinking Critically

There are at least two choices in every issue. In this case Chief Crowfoot can either stop the C.P.R. or allow the railroad-building through Blackfoot land to continue. There are good reasons for supporting each choice.

Law-related Concepts

1. Chief Crowfoot had a *legitimate (legal) reason* to refuse to allow the railway to be built across the reserve – "the treaty."

2. Chief Crowfoot was *responsible for making decisions* on behalf of his people.

3. In the treaty the Canadian government *kept the right* to build roads through the reserve.

4. The government and the C.P.R. were responsible for *settling issues through negotiations* with the Blackfoot.

Related Reading

1. Student journal entries from Lesson #1: "Chief Crowfoot's Problem."

2. Shared reading – Social Studies literature.

Activities

1. Shared reading of journal entries – "Chief Crowfoot's Problem" (from Lesson #1).

2. Begin class chart on board. Discuss "The Issue." What choices are available and what are some reasons for making each choice?

3. Students make journal entries in Chief Crowfoot role – "I think I should . . . because. . . ."

4. Display Class Chart – Chief Crowfoot's Choices (see Figure # 2).

Skills

1. Identifying an issue.

2. Identifying alternatives.

3. Developing the ability to adopt different points of view.

4. Making choices/decisions.

5. Reasoning to support decisions.

FIGURE #2: SAMPLE CLASS CHART – CHIEF CROWFOOT'S CHOICES

The Issue: The C.P.R. at Blackfoot Crossing

CHIEF CROWFOOT'S CHOICES

STOP THE C.P.R.	LET THE C.P.R. THROUGH
Initial Considerations	Initial Considerations
Uphold treaty rights	Violate treaty rights
Warriors show strength/pride	Warriors appear weak
Trains could cause fires	Trains bring food supplies
Duty to people who agreed to treaty	People might feel betrayed
Could lead to battle	Conflict during construction
Responsibility to defend people	Responsibility to provide for people

Lesson #3: The Alternatives

Thinking Critically

People's values influence their decisions (choices). People may make different choices because they hold different sets of values. Groups of people may share the same values and make the same choices.

Law-related Concepts

1. Chief Crowfoot could choose to stop the railway because he had the *right granted by the treaty*. He had many strong warriors who were not afraid to fight to protect their land.

2. Chief Crowfoot could choose to allow the C.P.R. to build across the reserve. In this way, he would act as a *responsible leader* by preventing conflict and ensuring food supplies for his people.

Activities

1. Students share their initial decisions through reading their journal entries from Lesson #2 – "I think I will . . . because. . . ."

2. Teacher-led group discussion of Figure 2: Class Chart.

3. Students are asked to reconsider their individual choices and list the most significant reasons for their choice. Tally and display results. See Figure #3: Sample Class Chart.
It is interesting to note that new reasons arise from the students' reflections.

4. Review graphing options (could be related to Math lesson) available to display tally:

   (a) Pictograph

   (b) Bar Graph

   (c) Line Graph

   (d) Circle Graph

5. Each student chooses and drafts a type of graph to represent class tally for both alternatives.

Skills

1. Speaking to different points of view.

2. Illustrating responses in a tally.

3. Organizing and prioritizing information.

4. Applying information to graphing procedures.

FIGURE #3: SAMPLE CLASS CHART – CLASS TALLY			
Let C.P.R. Through		**Stop C.P.R. Crew**	
Reasons	Tally	Reasons	Tally
1. Keep the treaty	////	1. War means heroes	
2. Blackfoot may gain more land	//	2. Preserve Indian rights	////////
3. New opportunities may arise	//	3. Fear of prairie fires	
4. Work for the Blackfoot		4. Be independent	
5. Make friends		5. Blackfoot can supply own food	
6. Save lives	////	6. Blackfoot "own" the land	
7. Food and supplies available	////////		
TOTAL	20	TOTAL	8

Lesson #4: Consequences

Thinking Critically

Before Chief Crowfoot could make a responsible decision on behalf of his people, he needed to consider the implications of the *consequences* of each choice.

☞ All choices have consequences that accompany them.

☞ Consequences can be considered by saying, "What would happen if I did. . . ?" and "What would happen if I did not. . . ?"

Law-related Concepts

Responsible citizens consider the *consequences* of alternative choices before making a final decision.

Activities

1. Group sharing of draft graph projects. Exchange ideas with whole class.

2. Class discussion – brainstorm implications/consequences of the two alternatives.

3. Journal entry (in role) – "I would/would not change my decision because . . ."

4. Display results of discussion on Class Chart – Consequences (see Figure #4) and record in notebooks.

5. Each student to produce "presentation" copy of graph.

Skills

1. Revision of drafts – adding and deleting after critical analysis and group feedback.

2. Hypothesizing consequences.

3. Analysing consequences.

4. Revising/altering opinions or choices after a consideration of new perspectives.

5. Confirming or establishing personal values.

6. Reflective writing.

FIGURE #4: SAMPLE CLASS CHART – CONSEQUENCES

What might happen if Chief Crowfoot stops the railway?	What might happen if he lets the railway through?
Blackfoot warriors and railway workers might fight each other.	Trains might cause fires on the reserve.
The government might stop sending food to the reserve.	Trains might bring food.
Settlers might go somewhere else.	Great numbers of settlers might arrive.
	Government might provide more land.

Lesson #5: Types Of Consequences

Thinking Critically

Consequences of choices can be positive or negative, long-term or short-term. Chief Crowfoot needed to consider all possibilities before making his decision.

Law-related Concepts

1. *Consequences of actions* affect individuals and the people they care about.

2. Consequences can be *positive* (good) or *negative* (bad). Many choices will have both positive and negative consequences.

3. Consequences may be *short-term* (immediate) or *long-term* (later/longer impact). Choices usually have both long-term and short-term consequences.

Activities

1. Class discussion – brainstorm hypotheses for positive/negative, long-term/short-term implications of consequences. Display in chart form – see sample (Figure #5)

2. Students make journal entry (in role) – "The consequences (positive/ negative, long-term/short-term) of my decision."

3. Group shares journal entries.

4. Share finished graphs – discuss procedures. (See Figures #6, #7 and #8.)

5. Shared reading of law-related literature.

Skills

1. Identifying main ideas.

2. Considering implications of actions on self and others.

3. Recognizing "dilemmas."

4. Recognizing that positive short-term consequences may have negative long-term consequences.

5. Evaluating and defending values.

FIGURE #5: SAMPLE CLASS CHART – TYPES OF CONSEQUENCES

Stop Railway	Let Railway Through
Consequences:	Consequences:
1. Blackfoot and railway workers may fight	1. Trains might cause fires
(+) might win, show power	(+) government concern
(–) might lose, many killed	(–) danger
(s.t.) risky	(s.t.) fear, anxiety
(l.t.) Blackfoot would be feared, distrusted	(l.t.) find ways of controlling

FIGURE #5: SAMPLE CLASS CHART – TYPES OF CONSEQUENCES

<u>Stop Railway</u>

Consequences:

2. Government might stop sending food
    (+)   learn to provide for ourselves
    (–)   many could starve
    (s.t.) hunger, fear of starvation
    (l.t.) might have to give up land for food

3. Settler might go elsewhere
    (+)   no threat to land
    (–)   government might lose interest in Blackfoot
    (s.t.) solve problem
    (l.t.) create more problems

<u>Key to Consequences</u>
    (+)   Positive
    (–)   Negative

<u>Let Railway Through</u>

Consequences:

2. Trains might bring food
    (+)   more food, sooner
    (–)   become dependent on train
    (s.t.) problem solved
    (l.t.) create new culture

3. More settlers might arrive
    (+)   possibility of more land
    (–)   overcrowding, conflict
    (s.t.) difficulties
    (l.t.) benefits for Blackfoot

    (s.t.) Short-term
    (l.t.) Long-term

FIGURE #6: SAMPLE PICTOGRAPH

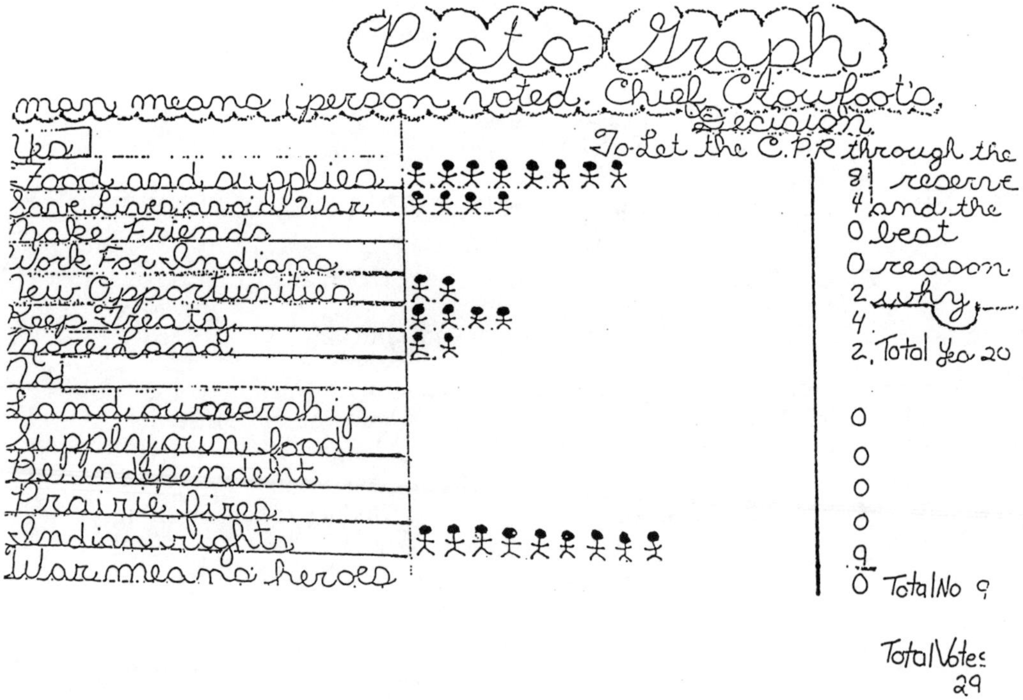

FIGURE #7: SAMPLE BAR GRAPH

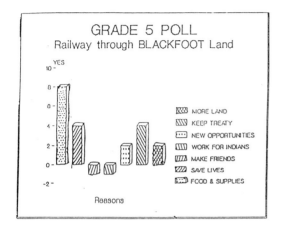
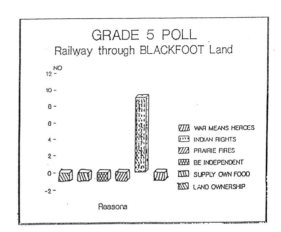

FIGURE #8: SAMPLE PIE CHART

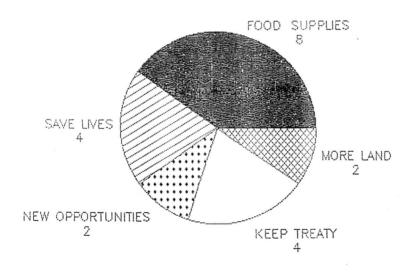

MAKE FRIENDS 0, WORK FOR INDIANS 0

Lesson #6: The Big Picture

Thinking Critically

Decisions are rarely either right or wrong. Choices usually have alternatives. Each alternative has positive and negative consequences as well as long-term and short-term implications. Chief Crowfoot needed to consider the "big picture" in order to make a responsible decision on behalf of his people.

FIGURE #9: CLASS CHART – THE BIG PICTURE

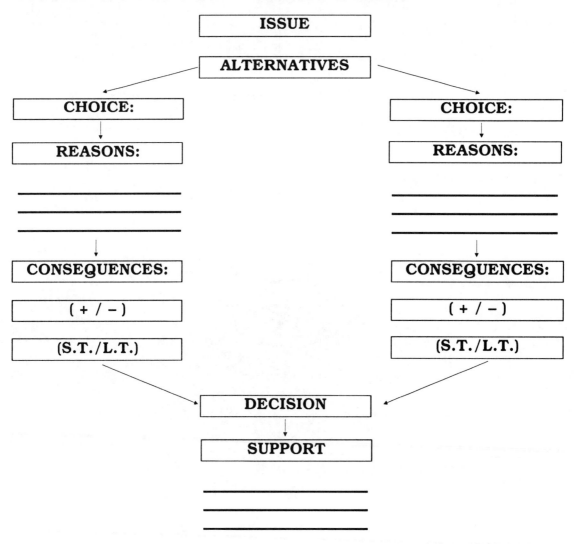

Law-related Concepts

1. *Responsible decision-making* requires logical consideration of alternatives and consequences.

2. A written decision or *"judgment"* describes the issue, the alternatives and the consequences or implications of each alternative.

Activities

1. Teacher-led class discussion and "mind map" – see Class Chart (Figure #9) to illustrate the "Big Picture" of the issue.

2. Discuss individual "Decision-making format" – class hand-out (Figure #10).

3. Students complete individual format for Chief Crowfoot's decision.

4. Each student (in character of Chief Crowfoot) writes a draft of their written judgment.

Skills

1. Synthesizing information for decision-making.

2. Note-taking.

3. Logical thinking progression.

4. Writing an argument.

5. Defending a position.

6. Writing a judgment.

FIGURE #10: CLASS HANDOUT
"THE BIG PICTURE" – DECISION-MAKING FORMAT

Issue: _____

Choice #1 _____	**Choice #2** _____
Reasons #1	**Reasons #2**
_____	_____
_____	_____
_____	_____
_____	_____
Consequences #1	**Consequences #2**
Positive_____	Positive_____
Negative_____	Negative_____
Short-term_____	Short-term _____
Long-term _____	Long-term _____

Decisions/ "Judgment" _____

Support/Justification _____

_____

_____

Lesson #7: So What?

Thinking Critically

Chief Crowfoot was a leader who was entrusted with making a responsible decision on behalf of his people. People in leadership positions have to make decisions on a regular basis.

Law-related Concepts

1. *Decision-making* is the responsibility of leaders.
2. *Group leaders, managers, parents, community leaders, politicians and law enforcement officials* have to make responsible decisions.

Activities

1. Group critique and feedback of draft judgments where applicable.
2. Individual activity – brainstorm positions of leadership requiring responsible decision-making.

3. Group sharing/class list of leadership positions.

4. Choose a "leader" to interview.

5. Discuss appropriate interview questions.

6. Revise judgments, prepare presentation version.

Skills

1. Evaluating leadership positions.

2. Posing questions.

3. Respecting others.

4. Constructive criticism – giving and receiving.

5. Organizing information.

Lesson #8: The Tribal Council

Law-related Concepts

Chief Crowfoot presented his *judgment* to his tribal council. This was the Blackfoot *"court of law."* In our culture, our *Justices* make decisions and present them in our courts of law.

Activities

1. Group sharing of final decisions. Select representatives to "sit around the council fire" for next lesson (Lesson #9).

2. Discuss recent legal decisions involving Native rights (e.g., land claims.) Students to do research – newspaper clippings, etc.

3. Individual research options:

    (a) Where is the closest court of law located?

    (b) Who works in the law courts? What are their jobs?

    (c) What kinds of issues are decided in courts?

    (d) What is meant by Provincial Court, Supreme Court, Court of Appeal?

4. Journal entry: "What I know/What I wonder about law courts today."

Skills

1. Public speaking.

2. Locating information.

3. Expressing opinions.

4. Making value judgments.

5. Defending value judgments.

Lesson #9: Rendering A Decision

Law-related Concepts

As their leader, Chief Crowfoot was *respected by his people and the tribal elders*. This respect was reflected in their *willingness to accept his decision*. Leaders must maintain their positions by being *worthy* of respect.

Activities

1. Student participants gather around the "council fire." Representatives from each group present their decisions (in role). Note: This activity lends itself to costumes and props and may be videotaped.

2. Class forum – feedback for the unit: "What we've learned," areas of personal interest.

3. Discuss individual "law court" research findings.

Skills

1. Self-evaluation.

2. Goal setting.

3. Public speaking.

4. Showing respect as an audience participant.

Lesson #10: Leadership Responsibilities

Thinking Critically

Responsibilities of leadership become greater as more people are involved. Different people have different values and different points of view. As a leader becomes *responsible to* more people, the difficulty of making responsible decisions also increases.

Activities

1. Discuss interviews with leaders – individual presentations. Plan "Bring a Leader to Class."

2. Choose a leadership role to adopt.

3. Students make journal entry: "As a (leadership role), I would be responsible to. . . . Some issues I would likely face are. . . . As a (leadership role), I would like to. . . ."

Skills

1. Writing from a different point of view.

2. Role playing.

3. Applying learning from one context to a different context.

CHAPTER 10
Exploring Law Through Forensic Science

Allan MacKinnon & Peter Williams

This chapter is a forensic science theme study on crime detection integrating many subject areas and school experiences.

Students at the intermediate level probably watch a lot of crime shows and so the activities in this chapter will likely be of great interest to them. Forensic science provides the opportunity for students to analyze a crime scene, gather evidence and conduct experiments to bring to light facts of a case from which they can draw conclusions about what happened and who is responsible. The evidence leads naturally to identifying a suspect, laying a criminal charge, finding corroborating evidence and seeking a legal resolution of the case. These are all important aspects of criminal law and of particular interest to intermediate students. The classroom activities presented here can be integrated in a variety of subject areas, including the sciences, humanities, fine arts and practical arts. Activities and teaching approaches have been designed for the upper elementary level, although some of the activities could certainly be adapted for the primary program, or, indeed, junior secondary or middle schools.

The learning activities related to science include:

✏ the science of detection,

✏ the properties and characteristics of substances, and

✏ means of classification and identification.

The learning activities related to the humanities include:

✏ experimenting with the "science of deduction"

✏ interpreting evidence

✏ gathering and researching information to support a position

- applying critical thinking skills
- making judgements about whether there is sufficient support for claims and accusations.

The learning activities related to fine and practical arts include:

- role playing a variety of professional experts
- interviewing and reporting
- preparing and examining legal documents
- preparing and defending a case in a mock trial
- making and supporting decisions relative to a legal issue

This theme study in crime detection is planned with *cooperative learning* strategies in mind. Students work in "home detective groups" of four or five individuals, each learning a different skill, or *expertise*, in forensic science. Later, when the groups are faced with a mock crime to solve, group members pool their expertise to collect and interpret the evidence before them – fingerprints, traces of hair and cloth, ink samples and the like – all to be presented to a jury in order to convict the guilty person(s), or prove the innocence of the accused. Above all, students and teachers alike should have fun throughout this theme study; the activities included in this chapter should be sufficient beginnings – from there, your imagination will suggest enjoyable and engaging extensions.

Students teaching students? It is as difficult and as easy as it sounds. In these changing times teachers want to teach school subjects in meaningful and relevant contexts of inquiry. One realistic method of helping to achieve relevance is through cooperative learning. Cooperation means working together to achieve a common goal. It should be clear that cooperative learning is not just putting students into groups and expecting them to learn on their own. Co-operative learning is **highly structured and has ground rules** – students must have social skills in order to work effectively in groups; they must have clear, predefined expectations; they must be motivated; and they must be interdependent.

One cooperative learning strategy is called **jigsawing.** As the word implies, jigsawing is putting all the puzzle pieces together to create a picture. There are many variations to the basic jigsaw pattern. In the basic jigsaw, as designed by Elliot Aronson, each student in a team specializes in one area of the learning unit, meets with students from other groups who are also specializing in that area, masters the material in the "expert group," and then returns to a "family group" team where the various expertise areas are shared. The Forensic Science Theme Study in Crime Detection is a cooperative learning strategy which uses a variation of the basic jigsaw technique.

Logistics of the Theme Study

Here is an example of how you might set up the theme study.

A crime is about to be committed at your school. A sample crime scene describing an incident and characters is provided at the end of the chapter. You may adapt this version to suit the interests and needs of your class or school. The sample crime involves school personnel including six teachers and the principal and so will require their cooperation as you set up the scene and identify the participants in the crime. Copies of resource materials can be found at the end of the Materials and Resources Section of the chapter along with instructions for copying and distributing. What follows is a description of the daily activities that constitute the Unit.

Day 1
Students Become Detectives

1. Divide the class into groups of four

2. Each group of four is a "Detective Agency".

3. Students name their Detective Agency and may create logos and put them on signs or business cards.

Detectives Select Expert Specialties

4. Each group member becomes one of the following specialists.

   a] Fingerprinting: taking and lifting fingerprints.

   b] Chemical Detection: identifying mystery powders, using paper chromatography to identify pen makes and candy types.

   c] Microscope Analysis: analyzing fiber, hair and torn materials.

   d] Track Analysis: soil analysis, making and identifying footprints.

5. Brainstorm about how these areas of expertise may be used to solve crimes.

Day 2
Experts Become Experts

1. Students meet in their Expert Groups (i.e., all finger printing specialists together, etc.)

2. Each Expert Group is given one copy to share of "Expert Group Work" lessons. (Found in the materials and resources section of this chapter)

3. One member of each expert group reads aloud to the other members of their group the procedures written in Lesson 1.

4. Expert groups discuss what the activity involves and how they will proceed.

5. Expert groups complete Lesson 1.

Day 3
Experts' Activities Continued

1. Expert groups complete Lesson 2

2. Expert groups prepare lesson plan to teach their specialty to the class.

3. Expert groups prepare a list of the materials they will need.

Day 4
Experts Teach the Class

1. Experts set up the materials they will be using when teaching.

2. Experts teach their specialty to the class (10-15 minutes each).

Teacher Preparation
The Crime Story, The Crime Scene

1. Prepare the "Crime Story." (You may use "Who Killed Roger Rabbit?" – See Materials and Resources section) The story may come from outside sources, another class of students or brainstorming among teachers.

2. Ensure that the "evidence" at the crime scene requires the four fields of expert analysis.

3. Brief the "suspects" about the Crime Story and if possible enlist their aid in setting up the Crime Scene (it will help them when they recount their part in the story during Detective interviews).

4. Set up the Crime Scene. NOTE: Students are not given access to the Crime Story. The point is for students to deduce what "really" happened by interviewing suspects and analyzing the evidence they find at the crime scene.

5. Determine how students will be presented with "the Crime" as well as the list of suspects. The following is an example of how one class of students was presented with the crime and the list of suspects:
   Students were shown a video (prepared by teachers, but could be other students) of a news program reporting "the crime" (the murder of Roger Rabbit). In this video, the school janitor (the first person on the scene) was interviewed. The janitor, in the process of recalling events at the school around the time of the murder, names the suspects. After the interview with the janitor, the news program shows a "clip" of the crime scene.]

Day 5
Experts Visit the Crime Scene

1. Students are presented with "the Crime" and a list of suspects (there are the same number of suspects as there are Detective Agencies).

2. Experts decide how they will go about collecting evidence at the crime scene as well as prioritizing the order of experts visiting the scene.

3. Expert groups visit the Crime Scene and collect the evidence which is relevant to their expertise. They should be careful not to interfere with other evidence.

Day 6
Analyzing the Evidence

1. Expert groups use their expertise to analyze the evidence which they collected at the scene of the crime, using the same procedures as they used in the Expert Work Group Lessons 1 and 2.

2. Each expert keeps notes about the evidence their Expert Group has collected as well as the results of their expert analysis (data) so that they may be able to present this information to their Detective Agency.

Day 7
Detectives Develop Hypotheses

1. Experts return to their Detective Agencies.

2. Experts present to their Detective Agencies both the evidence they collected at the crime scene and the results of the expert scientific analysis. One person acts as recorder of information.

3. The teacher assigns each Detective Agency one of the suspects to interview.

4. Before the interview, Detective Agencies brainstorm possible crime scenarios and develop a hypothesis in order to create a plausible line of questioning.

5. Students make up a list of:

   a. questions which they will ask their suspect during their interview.

   b. areas they would like to investigate for further evidence (classrooms of suspects, periphery of the scene of the crime etc.).

Day 8
Detectives Interview Suspects

1. Inform students that after interrogation of their suspects, each Detective Agency will report back to the class with information gained in the interviews.

2. Indicate the importance of keeping accurate and detailed notes of questions and responses, as well as noting anything "suspicious or interesting."

3. Each Detective Agency interviews a suspect, asking their prepared questions as well as asking any question that seems appropriate at the time.

4. Each Detective Agency may examine their suspect's classroom and/or other areas relevant to the crime and record this information.

5. Each Detective Agency presents to the class the information they gathered in the interview of their suspect.

Day 9
Detective Agents Become Police Officers and Officers of the Court

[At this stage students will need to change roles. Two students will become police officers and also serve as sheriffs in the courtroom. Two students will become lawyers serving as crown counsel or the prosecution team. Two students will become defense lawyers. One person will become a judge, another a court clerk. One representative from each Expert Group will become a specialist witness. The people involved in the crime (teachers and principal) may be called upon to testify in court. Twelve of the remaining students should serve as members of a jury. Remaining students can be assigned such roles as court reporter, journalists, photographers or courtroom artists.]

1. Two students appointed as police officers interview the members of the four Detective Agencies and develop a list of likely suspects. They decide who they are going to charge and then arrest the primary suspect.

2. The police inform the Crown Counsel and assistant of the charge and turn over the evidence against the accused.

3. The accused hires a lawyer and assistant to defend the case.

4. The Crown Counsel and his or her assistant interviews the representative from each expert group and other witnesses and develop the case against the accused. They determine who they will call to testify on behalf of the prosecution and issue subpoenas to the selected witnesses to appear in court on the day of the trial.

5. The defense lawyers interview the detectives, experts and witnesses and build a case to prove that their client is innocent. Defense lawyers decide who they are going to call to testify for the defense and issue subpoenas to the selected witnesses to appear in court on the day of the trial.

Day 10
Going to Court: A Mock Trial

1. The classroom is set up like a courtroom or a real courtroom can be booked for the mock trial. (See Court Proceedings at the end of Materials and Resources Section of this chapter). The teacher might consider inviting other classes to view the proceedings and arrange for legal robes to be worn by the judge and lawyers. The sheriff could also be in uniform.

2. The court clerk calls the court to order and announces the judge.

3. The judge calls for opening statements from the prosecution and the defense. (Three minute review of the facts of the case and suggestions as to why the accused is guilty or innocent of the crime.)

4. The prosecution then calls its witnesses. They question each witness in such a way as to reveal what happened at the time of the crime. At the end of the prosecution's questions the defense has the opportunity to question each of the prosecution's witnesses.

5. At the end of the prosecution's witnesses, the defense can decide whether or not the prosecution has a case against their client and whether they should proceed with their defense. If they decide to proceed, they call their witnesses to the stand and proceed to question them, the prosecution then can cross-examine the defense witnesses. The defense may or may not call the accused to testify, realizing that he too will be subjected to prosecution cross-examination.

6. When all of the witnesses have testified, the prosecution and defense give a brief summary of their cases to the jury.

7. The judge summarizes the law for the jury. He instructs them as to what constitutes first degree murder and on what basis they must make their decision.

8. The jury's job is to determine on the strength of the facts presented by the testimony whether or not the accused committed the crime that he has been accused of. They must come up with a unanimous decision. When they have finished their deliberations (which should be conducted in the presence of the rest of the class), they return to the courtroom and present their findings.

9. The judge either announces the acquittal and orders the release of the defendant or pronounces him guilty and sentences him according to the law.

MATERIALS LIST AND ACTIVITY RESOURCES

List of Materials for Expert Group Work

Equipment Check List
Equipment for each Lesson

Expert Group Lessons:	Photocopy one copy of each lesson and distribute to Expert Groups
	Fingerprinting – Lesson #1 and Lesson #2
	Fingerprinting – Data Recording Charts
	Chemical Detection – Lesson #1 and Lesson #2
	Chemical Detection – Data Recording Charts
	Microscope Analysis – Lesson #1 and Lesson #2
	Microscope Analysis – Data Recording Charts
	Track Analysis – Lesson #1 and Lesson #2
	Track Analysis – Data Recording Charts
Activity Resources:	Photocopy for participating teachers and principal
	Crime Story – "Who Killed Roger Rabbit?"
	The Suspects and the Clues
	The Murder Scene
	Letter to Participants
	Court Proceedings

Equipment check list:

- ☐ white paper
- ☐ yellow paper
- ☐ black paper
- ☐ filter paper
- ☐ pH paper
- ☐ chromatography paper (or filter paper)
- ☐ sugar
- ☐ salt
- ☐ corn starch
- ☐ baking soda

- ☐ dissecting microscopes
- ☐ funnels
- ☐ paper clips
- ☐ pencils
- ☐ scotch tape
- ☐ paint brushes with soft bristles
- ☐ fingerprint pads
- ☐ one permanent pen and a variety of water soluble pens, all black
- ☐ water
- ☐ vinegar

- ☐ talcum powder
- ☐ plaster of Paris
- ☐ clothespin
- ☐ candle
- ☐ candle holder (jar lid)
- ☐ stained J-cloth
- ☐ paper matches
- ☐ gum wrappers
- ☐ iodine solution
- ☐ test tubes
- ☐ test tube racks
- ☐ magnifying lenses or hand lenses
- ☐ microscopes
- ☐ ammonia
- ☐ tin foil
- ☐ pencil and lead powder
- ☐ fine graphite powder
- ☐ hair spray
- ☐ various cloth samples
- ☐ strands of fibre from woolen and silk scarves
- ☐ an assortment of hair samples, some fallen out, some pulled
- ☐ assorted candies with colored coatings: Smarties, M&M's, licorice allsorts, etc.
- ☐ potato chips
- ☐ microscope slides and cover slips
- ☐ black light (*ultra violet* lamp)
- ☐ a variety of soil types, collected from different areas

Equipment for each lesson: to be collected by teacher in advance of activity.

FINGERPRINTING

Lesson #1 : Classification, Identification and Matching Fingerprints

Equipment

- ☐ pencils
- ☐ scotch tape
- ☐ yellow paper
- ☐ white paper
- ☐ fingerprint pads
- ☐ magnifying lens

Background information

Fingerprints can be classified and identified according to their overall patterns and ridge characteristics. When attempting to identify the person who committed a crime the police rely on fingerprints because no two people have the same prints and prints at the scene can be matched to the finger prints of anyone suspected of having committed the crime.

Loop　　　Whorl　　　Arch

Classification

All prints can be divided into three pattern classes:

loops (60-65%) the loop can start from the right or left. Double loops have two loops (right and left) curling around each other.

whorls (30-35%) the print has a full circle at the centre.

arches (5%) clear arch shape around the centre; lines arch around.

You should find that your class will reflect this distribution.

Steps:

☞ Shade a part of the white sheet of paper with a pencil.

☞ Rub your left index finger on the pencil mark until the finger tip is covered with pencil lead.

☞ Put a piece of scotch tape over the finger.

☞ Peel the tape off and stick it to the yellow sheet of paper.

☞ Use a magnifying glass to examine the pattern of the fingerprint and compare it to the samples in the boxes.

☞ Mark below the fingerprint what type it is – "L" for loop, "W" for whorl, and "A" for arch. If the fingerprint seems to be a composite of more than one type, label it "C" for composite.

Make a chart showing the fingerprints of all the students in your expert group. Calculate the proportion of each type of fingerprint. Use a fraction or percentage to indicate the proportion of fingerprint type.

Fingerprint type	Number in Group	Proportion in Group
Loop		
Whorl		
Arch		
Composite		

Identification

Even on the same hand the fingerprints are not the same and can be used as a means of identification.

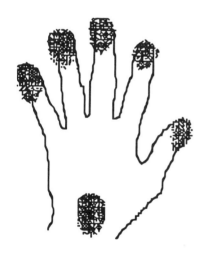

Steps:

☞ Trace the outline of your left hand on a sheet of yellow paper.

☞ Repeat steps 1 through 4 of Part 1 for each finger on the left hand.

☞ Place the tape on the correct finger of the outline, and identify and label each print.

☞ Make an extra copy of one of the fingerprints and put it at the bottom of the paper.

☞ Trade your paper with a partner and try to identify which finger the extra print came from.

Matching

The stamp pad activity is messy but closer to the type used by the police. After the challenge of finding another student who has a similar fingerprint, most students realize no two fingerprints are exactly alike.

Steps:

☞ Make a fingerprint record card similar to the one shown.

Name:			Date:	
Thumb	**Index**	**Middle**	**Ring**	**Baby**

- Ask a partner to roll your right index finger on the ink pad, then roll the inked finger on to the space on the card (you will have to practice this technique until you can produce a legible fingerprint).

- Repeat this method for each finger on your right hand.

- Examine each print with a magnifying glass and identify the pattern as in **Part 1**. Put this information on the card.

- Find another person who has a fingerprint similar to one of your own.

Lesson #2: Lifting and Developing Fingerprints

Lifting Fingerprints

Equipment

- ☐ talcum powder
- ☐ pencil and lead powder
- ☐ fine graphite powder
- ☐ scotch tape
- ☐ paint brushes with soft bristles

- ☐ paper clips
- ☐ white paper
- ☐ black paper
- ☐ potato chips

Background information

Latent fingerprints can be developed and lifted from a variety of surfaces and used for identification. *Latent* (a word derived from the Latin term meaning "to lie hidden") prints are made by the ridge designs of the fingers and thumbs which deposit oils, amino acids and salts on any surface. Generally, a search is always made for latent prints at the scene of a crime. In this activity the hidden prints are developed by applying colored powders to the surfaces. The powders adhere to the oil in the fingerprint. The color selected should contrast with the color of the surface. There are also chemical methods available for latent print development which rely on the reaction of chemicals with the amino acids or salts in the oils.

Developing Fingerprints

Steps:

Use white powder on dark surfaces   **Use black powder on light surfaces**

 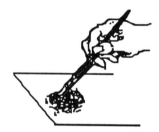

🖝 Rub your finger tips through you hair to make them oily (or handle a few potato chips). Press a finger on a flat, smooth surface.

🖝 Dust the print with a contrasting colored powder – white talcum powder for a dark surface, and black pencil powder or fine graphite powder for a light surface.

🖝 Brush the powder very lightly over the print. When the print starts to appear stroke it in the direction of the ridges.

🖝 When the fingerprint is fully developed press a piece of scotch tape on to the print.

🖝 Press down hard on the print and rub it well with a paper clip or your finger nail.

🖝 Peel off the tape carefully and stick it on to a piece of paper of contrasting color.

✎ Check the print against the record of it made in the first activity. Can you positively identify it?

Practice Lifting

Challenge someone from your expert group to find your fingerprint on an object and positively identify that it's yours. Practice your technique of "dusting" and "lifting" so that when you return to your home "detective group" your group members can depend on you as a *fingerprint expert*.

CHEMICAL DETECTION

Lesson #1: Mystery Powders

Equipment

☐ sugar

☐ salt

☐ corn starch

☐ baking soda

☐ plaster of Paris

☐ vinegar

☐ iodine solution

☐ tin foil

☐ black paper

☐ clothespin

☐ candle

☐ candle holder (jar lid)

☐ magnifying lens

☐ water

Background information

Each of the white powders have identifiable characteristics, if they are put to the proper tests. Some of these powders can be identified by physical means (e.g., heating to see if they melt, observing their crystals (sugar, salt), or comparing their "powderiness" on black paper). Other powders can be identified by chemical means (i.e., seeing how they react with things such as vinegar, iodine and water). If materials found at the scene of a crime can be traced to an individual, it increases the likelihood of convicting the culprit.

Powder Characteristics

Steps:

✎ Add a drop of vinegar to a small sample of each powder and record the results in the chart.

- Add a drop of iodine solution to a small sample of each powder and record the results in the table.

- Add a small amount of water (one or two drops) to each powder and record the results in the table.

- Spread a small portion of each powder on the black paper and observe with the magnifying lens. Record the results in the chart.

Test: Powder:	Vinegar	Iodine	Water	Black Paper	Heat
Sugar					
Salt					
Baking Soda					
Starch					
Plaster of Paris					

Heat a small amount of each powder in a tin foil cup (with a clothespin handle).

Safety Note:

Be sure to tie back long hair and roll up baggy shirt and sweater sleeves.

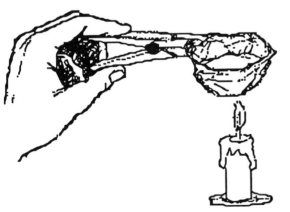

Record the results in the table.

Making Mystery Mixtures

Steps:

- Make a "mystery mixture" by combining small amounts of two or more powders.

- Divide the mystery mixture into two halves.

- Test one half yourself to make sure that all the required tests (to correctly identify the composite powders) work properly.

➥ For example, if you put some starch in the mystery mixture, then the mixture should turn dark blue, or black when a drop of iodine solution is added.

➥ Now, give the other half of your mystery mixture to another student in your expert group to see if he or she can detect the powders that are in it.

➥ Be sure that the appropriate evidence is presented when the solution to your mystery mixture is given. Use the chart to help organize your investigations.

MYSTERY MIXTURES	
Possible Powders *I think there is some . . .*	Observations and Deductions
sugar	
salt	
baking soda	
starch	
plaster of Paris	

Lesson #2: Paper Chromatography

Equipment

☐ chromatography paper (or filter paper)
☐ one permanent pen and a variety of water soluble pens, all black
☐ assorted candies with colored coatings: Smarties, M&M's, licorice allsorts, etc.

Background information

Chromatography is based on the fact that because molecules in ink (or other mixtures) have different sizes, charges, solubilities, etc., they travel at different speeds when they are pulled along a piece of paper by a *solvent* (in this case, water). For example, black ink contains several colors. When the water flows through a word written in black, the molecules of each one of these colors behave differently, resulting in sort of a "rainbow" effect. If a forensic scientist can prove that certain chemicals were present at the scene of the crime and the same chemicals were found on the person of the suspect, it increases the likelihood that the right person will be convicted. It may also help determine the time of the crime or whether a document is authentic or a forgery.

Separating Black Ink

Steps:

- ☞ Experiment with the effect of different pens on paper.

- ☞ Cut the filter paper into strips, one strip per marker.

- ☞ Place a dot of ink near the bottom of each strip. Be sure to identify which strip belongs to which pen. Dip the end of the strip into a container of water, just below the dot. Be sure the ink stays above the water, but the paper stays dipped into the water.

- ☞ Allow the water to soak up the strip and watch what happens to the ink drop. Compare each strip, once they are all finished. Repeat the experiment to determine if the results are consistent.

- ☞ Let the strips dry and tape them in your book as a record of the various pens.

Forgery Challenge

Steps:

- ☞ Write two identical notes using permanent ink.

- ☞ To "doctor" one, make small changes using a pen with water soluble black ink.

- ☞ Have the investigator (another student from your expert group) cut out individual letters from each note. (For example, the "o" in "hello" from each note.) Then tape the letters to the filter paper with the ink facing the filter paper and run the chromatography experiment to determine which note is authentic and which is a forgery.

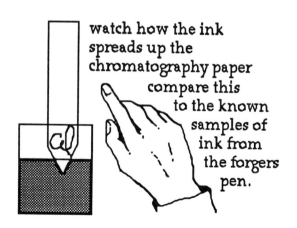

watch how the ink spreads up the chromatography paper compare this to the known samples of ink from the forgers pen.

- ☞ You may learn that the detection of a forgery by hand writing analysis is not really conclusive. You may need to prove a forgery by analyzing the ink used in making the forgery. For example, try forging the signature of one of the other members of your expert group. See if someone else can determine if the forged signature is authentic or not, simply by looking at it.

✏ Remember that many common inks are water soluble, and will therefore spread apart into their component dyes using water as a solvent in paper chromatography. If the ink you are testing does not spread using water, it may be "permanent" ink (meaning that it is NOT water soluble). In such cases, you would have to use a different solvent . . . perhaps something like rubbing alcohol, or paint thinner.

Other Uses of Chromatography

Chromatography is used to separate and identify all sorts of substances in police work. Drugs from narcotics to aspirin can be identified in urine and blood samples, often with the aid of chromatography. In this activity, you might practice your skill at paper chromatography by analyzing the candy coating of Smarties, M&M's, licorice allsorts and so on. You'll never know when you might need your skill at chromatography and detection to help sort out a crime.

Steps:

✏ Wet a Smartie and rub its candy coating on a piece of chromatography paper or filter paper.

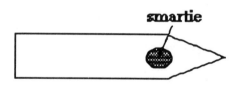

✏ Dip the "chromatogram" in water and observe the way the candy coating spreads across the paper with the water.

✏ Compare a number of different candy colors.

✏ Try the same with other brands of candy. Try M&M's, licorice allsorts, etc.

✏ You never know what a culprit will leave at the scene of a crime. Suppose that there was some candy left on the floor of a room where someone was murdered. What if you found a suspect with the same kind of candy in his/her pocket? What evidence could you provide to prove that the candy found on the suspect was from the same store as the candy found at the scene of the crime? Would chromatography come in to play here?

✏ Practice your technique using paper chromatography. Remember that you are now an "expert" in chemical detection. You may soon need your skills in analyzing white powders, the ink from pens or the coating on various brands of candy. Do you think you are ready to help your group solve a crime?

MICROSCOPE ANALYSIS

Lesson #1: Cloth Fibre and Hair Analysis

Equipment

- ☐ various cloth samples
- ☐ stained J-cloth
- ☐ hair spray

- ☐ hand lenses

- ☐ microscopes
- ☐ microscope slides and cover slips
- ☐ strands of fibre from woolen and silk scarves
- ☐ an assortment of hair samples, some fallen out, some pulled

Background information

Many crimes involve contact between the criminal and victim, resulting in cloth fibres and hair being left on the victim or at the scene of a crime. Also, the criminal may take fibres and hair from the victim away from the scene of the crime without knowing that he or she is carrying evidence. This physical evidence can be classified and identified by close examination techniques using hand lenses and microscopes.

Cloth Fibre Analysis

Steps:

- ✏ Look at a piece of cloth and record its color and texture. Draw what you observe.
- ✏ Use a magnifying glass to take a closer look at the cloth and record what you observe.
- ✏ Place a piece of the cloth on a microscope slide and examine the fibres. Draw what you observe under different powers of magnification and write a description of the material.
- ✏ Repeat steps 1-3 using a different piece of cloth. How can you tell the difference between the two?
- ✏ Now look at a stained J-cloth using the hand lens and the microscope. How can you describe the stain? Could you make a match if you had to?
- ✏ Use the charts to record your observations.

Observation Color and texture with	Cloth Sample 1	Cloth Sample 2	Stained J-Cloth 1	Stained J-Cloth 2
Eye				
Hand Lens				
Microscope				

Hair Analysis

Steps:

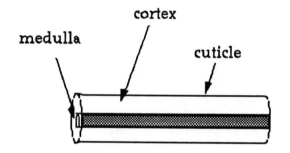

- Pull a few hairs from your head and put them on a microscope slide. Keep the hairs in place with a few drops of water and a cover slip.

- Use the microscope under low and high power to examine the hairs for the 3 main parts: the cortex (or main part of the shaft), the medulla (or central core of the hair), and the cuticle (or surface scale pattern). Draw a picture of what you observe.

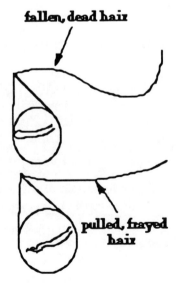

- Put some hair spray on a small part of your head (cover your eyes) and pull a few hairs to examine under the microscope. Do you see anything on the cuticle of the sprayed hairs?

- Compare your hairs to the hairs of other students in your expert group. See if you can get some of your teacher's hairs to compare. How could you make notes and records of the descriptions of the different hairs as you see them under the microscope?

- Notice that the ends of all of the hairs that you have pulled appear to be frayed on the end. If these hairs had fallen out, they would appear much differently.

✏ Use the chart below to practice drawing diagrams of the different hairs as you see them under the microscope. Practice describing the hairs as well.

Diagrams of hairs as seen under the microscope	Descriptions

Lesson #2: Putting the Pieces Together

Equipment

- ☐ tin foil
- ☐ gum wrappers
- ☐ paper matches
- ☐ black light (*ultra violet* lamp)

- ☐ hand lenses
- ☐ microscopes
- ☐ microscope slides

Background Information

One of the ideas behind forensic science is that a criminal always takes something away from the scene of a crime and leaves something behind. This might be something as simple as a part of a gum package. If the rest of the gum package found on a suspect matches the piece left at the scene of a crime, then a fairly convincing case can be put forward. Perhaps there would be a ripped piece of tin foil that would convict a suspect of a crime. Perhaps something as simple as a match left at the scene of an arson would be enough to convict a criminal, providing it could be physically matched to the book of matches found on a suspect.

Matching Torn Tin Foil

Steps:

- Tear a small piece of tin foil into two pieces.

- Carefully examine the torn surfaces of each half to determine if you can make a match. How would you record your observations and evidence in a convincing way?

- It may help to examine the torn edges under a microscope. Note that you will not be able to see anything under the microscope until you look at the edge of the tin foil. This should appear as a black jagged line between complete darkness and light (the tin foil is completely opaque – it does not allow any light to be transferred through it, so you cannot see through it under the microscope).

- Practice this technique using torn paper as well. Use the chart to help draw diagrams of the matching edges of torn paper and tin foil.

Can you match the two pieces
of torn tin foil?

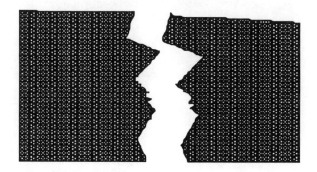

Does using the microscope help
in the "tough" areas?

one side of the tear   **the other side of the tear**

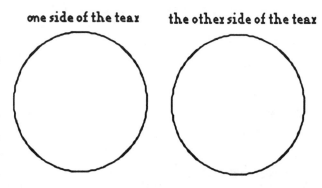

Matching the Parts of Gum Wrappers

Steps:

- Rip the top off a package of gum. Keep the package in your pocket and exchange the top with another student in your expert group. Examine the torn edge of the gum wrapper top that you get from another student.

- Draw a diagram of the shape of the tear of the gum wrapper top.

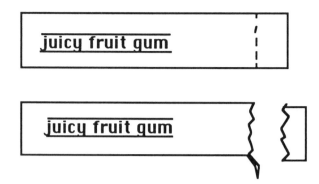

☞ Can you match this with the rest of the package that the other student has in his/her pocket? Make sure your diagrams are convincing enough to present to a jury.

Can you make a match?

Matching Matches

Background information

Safety Note:

Be very careful with matches. Do not try to light them. Not only can paper matches be compared to the books they came from, they can also be compared in terms of how they fluoresce under an ultra violet lamp.

Steps:

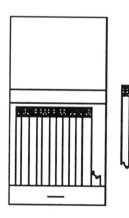

☞ Compare different paper match booklets under an ultra violet lamp (black light). You should notice that certain matches appear to give off more light than others under the black light (fluoresce).

☞ Tear off a match from one of the booklets. Challenge another student in your expert group to "match the match" to its booklet, in terms of both the torn surfaces and the way the match fluoresces under the black light.

Can you make a match?

☞ Can you put a convincing argument together? How must you prepare the "evidence"?

☞ Use the circles to help show that the match matches its booklet.

☞ How could you compare the way the match fluoresces? Can you make a "match" with the booklet where it came from?

194 Let's Talk About Law

Description of the way the match fluoresces	Description of the way the book fluoresces

TRACK ANALYSIS

Lesson #1: Soil Analysis and Footprint Analysis

Equipment

- ☐ white paper
- ☐ filter paper
- ☐ pH paper
- ☐ water
- ☐ vinegar
- ☐ ammonia
- ☐ a variety of soil types, collected from different areas

- ☐ funnels
- ☐ test tubes
- ☐ test tube racks
- ☐ magnifying lenses
- ☐ dissecting microscopes
- ☐ tin foil

Background information

Many crimes involve contact between the criminal and the victim resulting in soil from footwear and footprints being left at the scene of the crime. Or, sometimes the soil from the scene of a crime (say, a garden) can be found and identified on the suspect later (on shoes, in clothing, etc.). The physical evidence can be identified and classified. Also, the chemical composition can be used to compare soils and provide evidence that may help solve a crime.

Soil Analysis

Steps:

✏ Put a small amount of soil on a piece of white paper.

☞ Use the magnifying glass to find out the color(s) in the soil, the size of the soil particles, and any plant or animal life that is present.

☞ There may also be other things that can be found in a soil sample – for example, little bits of vermiculite, Styrofoam, pieces of paper, chips of wood and so on. All of these things can be characterized in a description of the soil.

☞ Feel if the soil is damp or dry.

☞ Practice analyzing, characterizing, and describing soil samples.

☞ Compare your soil to that of another student in your expert group.

☞ In what ways are the soils the same?

☞ In what ways are they different?

☞ Record all information on soil in this table.

Observations	Your soil	Partner's soil
color		
particle size		
plant life		
animal life		
other materials		
dampness		
pH (part 2)		

The Acidity of Soil

Steps:

☞ Set up three test tubes. Add 2 mL of water to the first, 2 mL of acid (vinegar) to the second and 2 mL of base (ammonia) to the third.

☞ Dip a piece of pH paper (litmus paper) into each of the liquids in the test tubes.

☞ Observe what happens to each of the pieces of test paper when it is placed in the neutral liquid (water), acid or base.

☞ Record your observations in the chart.

Sample	Red litmus paper	Blue litmus paper
Water (neutral)		
Vinegar (acid)		
Ammonia (base)		

✏ Put a small amount of the soil into a test tube. Add 10 mL of water and shake thoroughly to mix the soil and water together.

✏ Fold a piece of filter paper as shown.

✏ Place the filter paper in the funnel and filter the soil and water mixture into another test tube.

✏ Test the liquid that comes through the filter paper with the pH paper (litmus paper) to see whether it is acid, base or neutral.

✏ Record your results in the table in

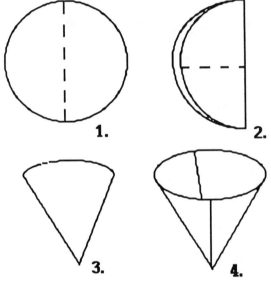

part 1. How can you tell the two soil samples from one another?

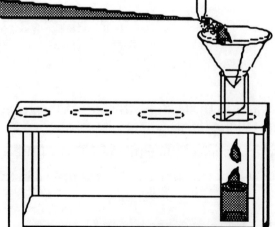

Lesson #2: Footprints Analysis

Background information

Shoes make very distinctive prints and often the brand can be determined by the print that it makes. As happened in the O.J. Simpson case, investigators can find out if the suspect owns or has ever purchased a shoe that matches the size and print found at the crime scene.

Steps:

☞ Push the print of your shoe into a piece of tin foil. You should be able to get a reasonably good replica of your footprint on the tin foil. Practice taking the measurement of the footprint and describing and drawing the pattern on the sole of the shoe.

☞ Compare your footprint with that of another student in your expert group. Can you describe the differences and similarities in the two footprints in a convincing way?

☞ You may be required to keep a tin foil record of your footprint, so be careful to do so. Remember that record keeping is very important!!

☞ Record your observations of footprints in the following chart.

Drawing of footprint	Description of footprint
Footprint 1	
Footprint 2	

☞ Practice comparing footprints again if you have extra time.

CRIME SCENE: AN EXAMPLE

Who Killed Roger Rabbit?

Roger Rabbit stopped by Cariboo Hill School to play his weekly game of poker with the guys. Every Monday night after school he would sit down to a card game in the staff room with Teacher 1, Teacher 2 and Teacher 3. The game started at 4:00 as usual. This week Roger had a large amount of money with him because he was going to buy his girl friend an engagement ring. But the game of poker didn't go well for Roger Rabbit this week, and by 5:00 he was losing badly. At 5:30 he excused himself from the game to go to the washroom. Since it was his deal, he took the cards with him so that he could mark the deck. The other players started to clean up the staff room while Roger was gone. Teacher 3 went down to the pop machine to buy a round of cola for the players.

In the washroom, Roger began marking the deck of cards. Suddenly, he realized that he would need more money in order to win back his losses, but he hadn't a penny left. Frantic and now desperate, Roger rushed down to the band room to pry open the safe and steal the auction money. In the midst of breaking into the safe, the Principal, who had been walking down the hall, saw Roger and began to dial the police for help. Just as the police answered the phone, Roger realized what was going on, drew a revolver from his pocket, and backed the Principal into the instrument room.

Along came the band teacher (Teacher 4) to close up her room and get ready to go home. Roger didn't notice her, as he had his back to the doorway of the instrument room. She saw what was going on and quickly looked around to find something she might use to save the Principal. There on an instrument cabinet was a plant. She grabbed it and struck Roger on the head with an heavy blow. The revolver fell on the carpet under a chair and Roger collapsed. He was out cold.

When she realized what she had done, Teacher 4 became hysterical. The Principal tried to calm her, but it was clear that she needed to get completely away from the sight of the unconscious Roger Rabbit. The Principal took her down the hall to get a drink of water.

Teacher 5 came into the music room to borrow an amp for his band. He saw the safe and stooped to examine how it had been pried open. All of a sudden he was jumped from behind. Roger had come to, and he was determined to grab the money from the safe and get out of there. First, he had to get rid of Teacher 5. There was a struggle and two shots were fired. Roger's body fell to the floor again, only this time he would not get up. There was a bullet in his heart. In a moment of panic, Teacher 5 quickly wrote a suicide note and signed it from Roger Rabbit. The note said that he had lost so much money gambling he could not bear to live any longer.

The Suspects and the Clues

Teacher 1:   Fingerprints are left on the playing cards found in Roger Rabbit's pocket. Because Teacher 1 was playing to the left of Roger, a few rabbit hairs are on Teacher 1's sweater. (Roger was so frustrated with the poker game that he started pulling out his hair.) Teacher 1 suffers from heartburn (soda on desk).

Teacher 2:   Fingerprints are left on the playing cards found in Roger Rabbit's pocket. Pieces of plaster board are found on Teacher 2's desk. (He's doing some renovations on his house, and he brought a small piece of plaster board from home to cut in the shop.) He chews the same gum as Teacher 6 and has an open package of it on his desk as well.

Teacher 3:   Fingerprints are left on the playing cards found in Roger Rabbit's pocket. While Teacher 3 was at the pop machine, he also opened a box of Smarties. Along came Teacher 5 on his way to the music room to borrow an amp. Teacher 3 offered Teacher 5 some Smarties, and the two stopped to chat. (Teacher 3 said that he was winning a lot of money in the poker game he was having with Roger Rabbit.) Later, the rest of the Smarties can be found on Teacher 3's desk.

Teacher 4:   Soil from the plant is tracked into her office. Her footprint is left in the spilt soil on the carpet in the music room. Her finger prints can be found on the cellophane wrap surrounding the plant pot that knocked out Roger Rabbit. Some of her hair is on the floor at the scene of the crime (she clutched her head when she became hysterical, and actually pulled out some of her hair).

Teacher 5:   The black felt pen used to write the suicide note is in his pocket. Some safe packing is in the cuff of a rolled up sleeve (from when he examined the pried open safe). There is rabbit fur on his pants and one smartie in his pocket.

Teacher 6:   Teacher 6 was in the school late on the day of the murder. She was preparing lessons for the next day. She had used the phone in the music room earlier and had opened a package of gum while she talked. She threw the top of the package in the garbage, and the rest of the pack is on the desk in her room. There is also a package of M&M's on her desk.

Principal: The next morning when he comes into the music room to see if Teacher 4 is alright, the Principal finds the other bullet fired from Roger Rabbit's gun. He puts it on his desk and plans to give it to the police when they come back for further investigation. His footprints are also left in the soil on the floor of the music room, and some of the soil is still on his shoes (and can be found under his desk).

Note: Several suspects have a black felt tipped pen in their possession during the time when the evidence is being gathered.

The Scene of the Murder

Roger Rabbit's body is outlined in tape on the floor beside the instrument room. In the area of Roger's heart, there is a single bullet lying on the floor, left behind after the dead 'toon vaporized. There is some safe packing found on the floor near the door of the body. Also, there are several crushed Smarties on the floor. There are rabbit hairs and traces of soil found all over the scene of the murder. The suicide note is lying beside the area where the body was, and the gun has disappeared as well.

Nearby in the instrument room there is a spilt plant on the floor with footprints in the soil (Teacher 4 and Principal's). There is the top of a gum wrapper on the floor beside the knocked over garbage can (matches the rest of the package found on Teacher 6's desk). Rabbit hair is found on the floor by the plant, along with several strands of Teacher 4's hair. Also, Teacher 4's finger prints are all over the cellophane wrap surrounding the plant pot.

On the news, there is a view of the scene of the crime and a description of what was found there. A neighbor from a nearby house reports having heard two shots at 5:36 p.m. The custodian explains that this is what was found in the morning when the school was opened up. "It's too bad. I know how much he liked playing poker with some of the teachers here." The custodian explains that there was no body to clean up because 'toons vaporize when they die. "The only thing left was the bullet that killed him. Even the gun disappeared." The custodian reports having left the school at 5:30, but remembered that there were still seven people (besides Roger) who were still in the school at that time – the Principal and Teachers 1-6. The announcer notes that police have asked for any assistance they can get in solving the crime.

Letter to the Suspects

(date)

Dear Suspect,

There has been a murder at _____ School! Roger Rabbit has been killed, and guess what? . . . you are one of the seven suspects.

Please read the scenario and plant the evidence on yourself and / or your desk in time to be interrogated by a small group of students (_____'s Science Class) on (date / time).

Thank you for your help!! Please answer the students' questions according to the scenario. (Don't fabricate any further fantasies.) We'll see if the "Detective Teams" can solve the crime by gathering and interpreting the evidence according to the scenario laid out here.

Again, thank you for your cooperation . . . and have fun.

By the way, the trial will be on (date).

Court Proceedings:

Sheriff:	All rise, this Court is now in session. His/her Honor Judge _____ presiding. (Everyone remains standing until the Judge tells them to be seated.)
Judge:	You may be seated
Court Clerk:	The case of the Queen versus _____
Judge:	Thank you. Are all parties present?
Crown:	(Stands and addresses the Judge.) Yes, Your Honor. I am _____ and these are my learned friends _____ and _____. We are acting on behalf of the Crown.
Defence:	(Stands and addresses the Judge.) Yes, Your Honor. I am _____ and these are my learned friends _____ and _____. We are acting on behalf of the accused.
Judge:	Thank you. (To court clerk.) Please read the charge. (Judge addresses the accused.) Please rise to hear the charge. (The accused, the defence lawyers and the Court Clerk rise.)
Court Clerk:	_____, you are charged with murder in the first degree in the death of Roger Rabbit on (date) at (time) and (place). How do you plead?
Accused:	Not guilty
Court Clerk:	Your Honor, the accused pleads "not guilty"
Judge:	(Addresses the Crown.) Please proceed with your case.
Crown:	(Opening Statement.) . . . We now wish to call our first witness, _____
Court Clerk:	Take the Bible in your right hand. Do you swear to tell the truth, the whole truth and nothing but the truth, so help you God?
Witness No. 1:	I do. (Crown proceeds with their questions.)
Judge:	Does the Defence wish to cross-examine this witness?
Defence:	Yes, Your Honor. (Stands and questions Crown Witness Number 1.) (This procedure follows for each Crown witness.)
Judge:	(To the Crown.) Do you wish to call any more witnesses?

Crown:	No, Your Honor. We rest our case.
Judge:	(To Defence.) Would the Defence please begin?
Defence:	(Opening Statement and informs the Court which witnesses will be called for the Defence.)
Court Clerk:	(Calls the witnesses in turn swearing each of them in as before. Defence conducts its examination and each witness may be cross-examined by the Crown.)
Defence:	(Completes its case.) We rest our case, Your Honor.
Judge:	(Invites Defence to begin their Closing Statement.)
Defence:	(Closing Statement to Jury.)
Judge:	(Invites the Crown to give their Closing Statement.)
Crown:	(Closing Statement to Jury.)
Judge:	(Instructs the Jury.)
	(Jury leaves to decide on their verdict. It is more interesting for the audience if the jury deliberates in their presence.)
	(Jury returns.)
Judge:	Ladies and gentlemen of the jury, have you reached your verdict?
Jury Foreman:	Yes, Your Honor, on the charge of first degree murder, we find the accused (guilty/not guilty.)
	(The Judge lets the accused go free if the verdict is not guilty. If the verdict is guilty . . .)
Judge:	Would the Crown please speak to the Sentence.
Crown:	(The Crown will be prepared to suggest a suitable Sentence, in their opinion.)
Judge:	Thank you. Would the Defence please speak to the Sentence.
Defence:	(The Defence will be prepared to suggest a suitable Sentence, in their opinion.)
Judge:	(Sentences the accused.)
	This court is now adjourned.
Court Clerk:	All rise, this court is now adjourned. (Everyone stands while the Judge leaves.)

This chapter has gone through a long development process involving many curriculum developers and educators beginning with the work of Peter Williams of the Toronto Board of Education. Margaret Scarr and Gary McKinnon of the Burnaby School Board provided valuable suggestions, and sponsored one of the first trials of this unit in B.C. Special thanks go to Jeff Caughlin and the staff of the Vancouver R.C.M.P. Forensic labs for their assistance and ideas. Colleagues at Simon Fraser University have helped to build on the interdisciplinary aspects, as well as the emphasis on education, society and the law.

PRINTED AND BOUND
IN BOUCHERVILLE, QUÉBEC, CANADA
BY MARC VEILLEUX IMPRIMEUR INC.
IN APRIL, 1998